PENGUIN BOOKS

VERA BRITTAIN

Hilary Bailey was born in 1936 and lives in London. She has written four novels, *Polly Put the Kettle On*, *Mrs Mulvaney*, *All The Days of My Life* and *Hannie Richards*. She reviews fiction for the *Guardian*.

'I must have discovered Vera Brittain quite early,' she writes, 'because I can remember reading *Honourable Estate* with my feet in the garden pond! I'm pleased, now, to have been able to find out more about this very interesting woman some forty years after having first made her acquaintance.'

LIVES OF MODERN WOMEN

General Editor: Emma Tennant

Lives of Modern Women is a series of short biographical portraits by distinguished writers of women whose ideas, struggles and creative talents have made a significant contribution to the way we think and live now.

It is hoped that the fascination of comparing the aims, ideals, set-backs and achievements of those who confronted and contributed to a world in transition, and the high quality of writing and insight will encourage the reader to delve further into the lives and work of some of this century's most extra-ordinary and necessary women.

Hilary Bailey

Vera Brittain

Penguin Books

Penguin Books Ltd, Harmondsworth, Middlesex, England
Viking Penguin Inc., 40 West 23rd Street, New York, New York 10010, U.S.A.
Penguin Books Australia Ltd, Ringwood, Victoria, Australia
Penguin Books Canada Limited, 2801 John Street, Markham, Ontario, Canada L3R 1B4
Penguin Books (N.Z.) Ltd, 182–190 Wairau Road, Auckland 10, New Zealand

Published in Penguin Books 1987
Copyright © Hilary Bailey, 1987
All rights reserved

Grateful acknowledgement is made to the Literary Executors of Vera Brittain's Estate
for permission to use extracts from Vera Brittain's published works.

Made and printed in Great Britain by
Richard Clay Ltd, Bungay, Suffolk
Set in Monophoto Photina

For Geoffrey Handley-Taylor

CONTENTS

Ready Division of Archives and Research Collections, McMaster University, Hamilton, Canada)

Vera, in pyjamas, when a VAD in Malta (1916) (The William Ready Division of Archives and Research Collections, McMaster University, Hamilton, Canada)

Vera in VAD uniform, Malta (1916) (The William Ready Division of Archives and Research Collections, McMaster University, Hamilton, Canada)

Vera and some of her patients at St George's Hospital, Malta (1916) (The William Ready Division of Archives and Research Collections, McMaster University, Hamilton, Canada)

Wounded soldiers in France, waiting for transport to a base hospital similar to the one at Etaples (1916) (The Trustees of the Imperial War Museum, London)

Winifred Holtby and Brigne (1921) (The William Ready Division of Archives and Research Collections, McMaster University, Hamilton, Canada)

Wedding of Vera Brittain and George Catlin (1925) (Courtesy of Mr B. C. Wood. Photo, Bodleian Library, Oxford)

Vera with John and Shirley (c. 1932) (The William Ready Division of Archives and Research Collections, McMaster University, Hamilton, Canada)

Winifred Holtby (early 1930s) (Courtesy of Paul Berry. Photo, Elizabeth Ivimey. From Hull Local Studies Library)

Vera Brittain, aged forty-three (1936) (Photo, Howard Coster. National Portrait Gallery, London)

Vera at Winifred's grave (1954) (Courtesy of Paul Berry. From Hull Local Studies Library)

Vera and George (1954) (Photo, Mark Gerson)

ACKNOWLEDGEMENTS

My thanks are due to Livia Gollancz, who generously let me borrow the manuscript of *Chronicle of Friendship* before publication, and to my diligent research assistant, Kate Moorcock. I must also thank Mark Bostridge, who, with Paul Berry, is writing a biography of Vera Brittain to be published by Chatto and Windus in 1988, for his very useful comments and corrections of my manuscript, the Vera Brittain Estate, and, especially, Geoffrey Handley-Taylor, joint executor of the Vera Brittain Estate, whose kindness while I was writing knew no measure.

1893	Vera Brittain born in Newcastle-under-Lyme, daughter of Thomas and Edith Brittain.
1895	Edward Brittain, Vera's brother, born. Roland Leighton born.
1914	Vera goes to Somerville College, Oxford.
1915	Leaves to join V A Ds. Roland Leighton killed in action.
1916	Vera nursing at Etaples, France.
1918	Edward Brittain killed in action.
1919	Vera returns to Oxford to study history.
1921	Vera graduates from Oxford.
1922	Vera and Winifred Holtby set up house together.
1923	Vera's novel *The Dark Tide* published.
1924	Vera's second novel, *Not Without Honour*, published.
1925	Vera marries George Catlin and goes with him to the USA.
1926	Vera returns permanently to Britain.
1927	Vera and George's son, John, born.
1930	Vera and George's daughter, Shirley, born.
1933	Vera's autobiographical *Testament of Youth* published.
1935	Vera's father, Thomas Brittain, dies.
1936	Winifred Holtby dies. Vera's novel *Honourable Estate* published.

1940	Vera's book about Winifred Holtby, *Testament of Friendship*, published.
1940	Children leave for the USA.
1942	Pacifist book, *Humiliation with Honour*, published.
1943	Children return to Britain.
1945–7	Visits in Europe, also in the USA.
1948	Vera's mother, Edith Brittain, dies.
1949–51	Vera Chairman of the Peace Pledge Union.
1949–50	Visits India and Pakistan.
1957	Vera's autobiographical book *Testament Of Experience* published.
1965	*Envoy Extraordinary*, life of Mrs Pandit, published.
1970	Vera Brittain dies.

ONE

The Great War

'Long argument on and off most of the day with George and Winifred,' wrote Vera Brittain in her diary in 1932, 'about whether it was best to be born a member of the cultural aristocracy or be like Winifred and myself, forced to make one's way out of a wrong environment into a right one and become a little vulgar in the process.' Putting forward her own arguments, she goes on, 'Personally I cannot think it anything but an incomparable advantage to have been absorbing Platonic philosophy and acquiring a respect for scientific truth at an age when I was wasting my time by reading Longfellow and Mrs Henry Wood, while Winifred endeavoured to find scope for the activity of her mind in lavatory copies of the *Ladies' Realm*.'

She was then thirty-nine. The argument took place immediately after she finished *Testament of Youth*, her personal history of the First World War, the book which made her famous and by which she is still most remembered today. In the early portion of the book she was also brooding about her background: 'how many of my present-day friends,' she asks, 'were themselves limited by a horizon as circumscribed as that which bounded my first thirteen years?' 'Not many' is the answer she expects, and it is true certainly that although her parents were prosperous, respectable, thoroughly kindly people, who, in the end, never stopped her from doing what she felt she had to do, they were by no means cultured or intellectual – they might not even have felt very flattered if anyone had suggested they might be. The Brittains were a Staffordshire family, Vera's maternal grandfather, John Bervon, was Welsh. It had been her father's grandfather who had gone into the paper-making trade, centred on Leek in Staffordshire, and built it up, with Victorian grit and determination, into the prosperous business it became. If there is any truth in the idea that it is more normal for children to resemble their grandparents than their parents, then it may well be from this forceful ancestor that Vera Brittain inherited the single-mindedness, foresight and willingness to work long hours and endure many hardships to achieve what she wanted – and also perhaps the sheer drive to take herself out of the situation into which she was born and into the world she felt she should inhabit. Thomas Brittain, her amiable but melancholic father, and Edith Brittain, his devoted but anxious wife, do not seem to have been the parents to hand on or foster these qualities.

Vera was their first child, born in a small house in Newcastle-under-Lyme in December 1893. Less than two years later her brother Edward came along and the Brittain family was complete. The family moved to a larger house in Macclesfield, then, when Vera was eleven, to Melrose, a large, comfortable house in Buxton, Derbyshire – the kind of tranquil house with long lawns, tennis courts and many servants which we think of as typically Edwardian. It is almost as if the Brittains had moved into the kind of house the peace of which was classically destined to be destroyed by war. By 1915, twelve years later, they had moved south and were never to live like that again.

Meanwhile Vera enjoyed both the benefits and disadvantages of a childhood spent as the only daughter of a well-off Midlands industrial family. She records that there were less than a dozen books in the house in Macclesfield – just a few novels and some books on paper-making which were kept on a window-ledge behind the sitting-room curtains. Among these volumes, too, was the only source, apart from the Bible, of sex education for the respectable middle-class children of the time: the family medical book. It was not a good intellectual start for this gifted child but it was probably only her later contact with the literary world of London – that close-knit world of blood, family friendship and old school and university alliances all springing from a cultured middle and upper-middle class, mainly based on the South of England – which made her conscious of the kind of background she lacked.

However, if the Brittains' only daughter was not given much in the way of high birth or cultural advantage at her christening, the Good Fairy did provide basic essentials: health (she never had a major illness), strength, an unusual amount of stamina, a strong intelligence and, as bonuses, determination, mental and physical courage and considerable good looks. Small – she was 5' 3" – with dark hair, a clear complexion and eyes hovering between violet and brown, she was a very pretty girl and remained an attractive woman well into middle age. She was also rather vain and believed it was a duty, as well as a pleasure, to pay attention to her appearance. 'An even more ghastly exhibition than usual of sartorial monstrosities' she writes of the women she found at a reunion of old Somerville graduates.

About her undoubted physical courage she was more offhand. Having gone out to Malta to nurse during the First World War she speaks of possessing 'a modicum of courage'. Writing of her experiences during the blitz, she mentions her 'natural cowardice'. It is hard to believe in this cowardice: really nervous people are not usually to be found regularly offering themselves up to danger. Perhaps neither Thomas nor Edith Brittain were ever fully aware that they had given birth to two similar children, who were both nervous, sensitive, gifted and capable in adult life of considerable physical bravery.

The maternal side of Vera's family, the Bervons, were musical and obviously intelligent – Vera's aunt was joint headmistress of the school she attended in the days before the First World War. Throughout her life the Brittains' only daughter seems to have shown signs of trying to balance the sober, methodical, fairly unimaginative person she could easily be with the fiery, idealistic, deeply romantic individual she could also be at other times. She hated Buxton and despised her own rather stuffy, provincial background, but she could never forget its rules. Maintaining order, regularity and self-control, establishing a good reputation in the world, looking after children properly and working hard were standards she seldom, if ever, questioned. She may not have followed the patterns of her class and sex – she led a less than conventional life – but what she did she managed after the style of Buxton, not Bohemia. And it was Buxton, too, which gave her that safe, if somewhat suffocating, upbringing which is so often a springboard to action in later life. She also had financial security. Although she wanted to be self-supporting and generally was, she never had to fear what would happen to her or her children if all failed: an even more important consideration in those pre-Welfare State days than it would be today.

Health, wealth, intelligence, good looks and family stability are what the Good Fairy traditionally brings to the christening. In real life the Bad Fairy usually attends too, even if only to translate some of the advantages into disadvantages. For although everything in Vera's account of her own childhood speaks of safety, none of it says anything about happiness. Thomas Brittain seems to have suffered for a large part of his life from what was described (by Winifred Holtby) even as late as the 1930s by the old-fashioned word 'melancholia', which we would now call depression. His wife obviously had to spend much of her time easing his attacks of unhappiness and anxiety, and usually if one individual in a household, especially if it is the head of the house, suffers in this way it casts a general pall over everybody. There were, of course, no analysts and no drugs to help the average sufferer in those days. This illness of her father may have affected Vera in the form of a considerable degree of anxiety and constant self-demands – conditions which tend to get worse as the individual gets older. Her early life, prosperous and comfortable as it was, can have given her little sense of fun. It seems to have been a world of thick carpets, long faces, respectable behaviour and family quarrels. The advantage may have been that it equipped Vera and her brother better than many of their contemporaries for the horrors of the war, when it came. A gloomy parent, full of dire warnings and predictions, at least prepares a child for the worst, and the worst was what the Brittain children, and the rest of their generation, were destined to meet.

Both brother and sister were given a solid education, although the brother's, naturally, was more solid. Edward went to a public school, Uppingham, in Leicestershire. At thirteen Vera went to a boarding school in Surrey presided over by her mother's sister. Edward was intelligent and also gifted musically. He played the violin and composed, perhaps a legacy from the Bervons. Thomas Brittain always hoped he would run the family firm but, after discussion of whether he should take the exams for the Indian Civil Service, it was later agreed that he would go to Oxford and read Greats, though Edward himself had other plans and intended to add music to his studies.

In spite of the family disagreements about what he should do, when he left school Edward had at least three options, all of which had been discussed. Vera, as the Brittains saw it, had one, which had never been discussed. After she left school in 1912 she would stay at home until a suitable husband appeared, and then marry. Since she was well brought-up and charmingly small and pretty, there was no reason why she should not make a respectable match in the circles in which the Brittains moved. So at this stage, at eighteen years old, she was reduced to the depressing and humiliating experience of middle- and upper-class girls known as 'helping mother at home' – a euphemism for waiting for a husband, since 'mother', who would usually have servants and grown-up children, was probably less in need of help than she had ever been. 'Helping' would not be a matter of scrubbing floors and doing the family laundry, but of counting the sheets, arranging the flowers and changing library books. There would be tennis and tea parties. It was a stultifying life for an energetic girl. There was little to do and moreover the girl knew she was on offer but had, of course, to pretend she was unaware of the fact. Both Vera herself and her friend Winifred Holtby recall the situation with loathing in novels they wrote. It has to be remembered that speed in this business was important. Up to just a few years ago women congratulated themselves on having married at eighteen or nineteen years old. In the highly commercial business of marriage, getting snapped up early was a sign of success and the shelf life of a woman was not a long one – a woman who reached twenty-five without marrying was a worry to herself and to her relations. By thirty the game was more or less over. During their marriageable years, if at no other, the life of working-class women might have been preferable. There were, of course, very few suitable jobs for young women of Vera Brittain's standing and those that there were, such as teaching, were ill-paid. Certainly it would have been unthinkable for anyone who could afford to keep a daughter at home to have let her take a job. The other sorts of job, those done by working-class women, were hard and even more badly paid. To see the situation clearly we have to imagine a society where a third of the work-force was female. Out of every 100 employed women at that time fifty would be domestic servants, twenty-five would work in mills or textile factories, six would be sales assistants in shops, three clerical workers, perhaps typists, and only *one* would be either self-employed (probably a shop owner) or belong to the higher professional classes.

With nothing to do but play tennis and go to dances, after over a year Vera found the only way out. She would go to Oxford. In *Testament of Youth* she describes the angel who came to point the path as 'an old family lawyer', which sounds very respectable. It was more a matter of Vera dragging her mother, who had to chaperone her, to a series of University Extension lectures in Buxton, impressing the lecturer, John Marriott, and then, when he came to spend the night with the family, using his remarks about Vera's education as ammunition against her mother and father. Thomas Brittain had already refused to spend a penny more on his daughter's education but, respecting John Marriott's opinion, he decided she should be allowed to take the Oxford examinations, encouraged by a belief that the student could choose to go for only a year if she wanted. For a long time no one seems to have disabused him of this impression.

Vera arrived in Oxford in the summer of 1913 to check the possibilities, surprising the Principal of Somerville by appearing for her appointment in the evening in an evening dress and cloak – the first but not the last time she was to scandalize the female intelligentsia with her smart clothes.

She was advised not to try for a scholarship, but decided to do so anyway. From that point her life as a flower-arranger and attender of tennis parties was over. Cramming for the Oxford scholarship exam in English she got up at six and studied until lunch-time in a room in which, she claims, there was never a fire as it was against household rules to light one there. Somehow it is hard to imagine the kindly and conscientious Edith Brittain, in a household where there were three maids, maintaining this rule for very long. In March 1914, at the age of twenty, she took the Somerville exam and was awarded an exhibition. Although less prestigious than a scholarship, it was a remarkable achievement for a young woman who had been studying virtually alone for nine months, and who was in competition with others who were probably still at schools much tougher academically than the one she had attended. She had not only set herself on an entirely different path now, but was completely vindicated. There was one more minor examination to pass in the summer and she would be on her way.

Backtracking, it still seems extraordinary that she should have conceived and carried through an idea so unlike anyone else's. 'How *can* you send your daughter to college, Mrs Brittain?' said one woman to Vera's mother. 'Don't you want her ever to get *married*?' Of course, Vera was desperate, which helped. All she had ahead of her was the prospect of a marriage like her parents'. She had scanned the young men who would offer her this and found them lacking. Vera certainly wanted to marry, but not in Buxton on Buxton terms. But in one respect the times were on her side. Although the Brittains seemed unaffected, the position of women had changed and was changing.

Vera was ten when Emmeline Pankhurst started the Women's Social and Political Union to campaign for the vote. By 1913, political methods having failed, the disappointed women started what we would now call a terrorist campaign – they smashed windows, slashed pictures and set fire to buildings; they put a bomb in Lloyd George's house. By the end of the year they had done an estimated £500,000 worth of damage, which (it is difficult to calculate exact values) might be tens of millions today. The authorities, who had not been gentle with the women during their ordinary demonstrations, responded with more violence. The story of brutal arrests, imprisonments and forcible feeding is well known. Curiously enough, Vera, although later a feminist, mentions nothing of this in her girlhood diaries, but there can have been no way, in a household which took a daily paper, of not knowing about the suffrage movement. In the same month that Vera was in Oxford discovering how she could get a place, Emily Davidson threw herself under the King's horse during the Derby as a protest on behalf of the suffragettes. She was killed. By 1914 the Prime Minister, Herbert Asquith, had in fact committed himself to introducing a bill in Parliament offering women the vote. But long before this the lives of women like Vera had been subtly transformed by the knowledge of the struggle.

Vera was also helped by her brother Edward's unfailing support. When the family suddenly decided, after the examinations, that she should in fact *not* go to Oxford, he simply said that if that was the case he would not go himself. His very existence was probably a spur to Vera's ambitions.

A family with a paper mill to pass on must have rejoiced when the second child mercifully turned out to be a boy, not another girl. An intelligent child who sees her little brother taken more seriously than she is but who knows that in the real business of life she is his superior – she has to do up his shoes and find his hat – may well become very ambitious. However much she loves him – and Edward and Vera were best friends throughout – it will certainly take a great deal to persuade her she is inferior because of her sex. The older sister of a younger brother can easily become a subversive from childhood on. If Edward, her younger brother, was going to Oxford, Vera may have reasoned, why shouldn't she?

As if the exam success, destined to take her away from the life of a marriageable girl living at home, were not enough, the previous spring Vera had met the young man whose life and death were to transform the rest of her life. If there had been no Roland Leighton it is safe to assume there would have been no *Testament of Youth* and no Vera Brittain as we know her.

Although she says in *Testament of Youth* that the first meeting between herself and Roland Leighton was in 1914 when he came back with Edward from Uppingham to stay during the Easter holidays, in fact, according to her journal, they had met the previous summer at the school, when she mentioned him casually as a friend of her brother. But a *coup de foudre* is no *coup de foudre* if the couple have met earlier and at least one of the couple has taken no notice of the other. And even during their official first (actual second) encounter, her account in *Testament of Youth*, written fourteen years later, indicates a higher level of interest than her on-the-spot journal does. One reason was that Vera had dropped into the classic trap of the bored young woman at home and had half fallen in love with the vicar, a married man, a story she tells in her novel *Not Without Honour*. Besides, Roland was eighteen, a year and a half younger than she was, the contemporary of her younger brother and still at school. However, they got to know each other better during Roland's stay at Buxton. When he left he sent her a key work, from which she was still quoting during times of emotional crisis when she was forty years old: Olive Schreiner's *Story of an African Farm*. It is the tale of two girls on a farm in South Africa, one of whom, Lyndall, is passionate, intelligent, unconventional but nevertheless doomed. The book was something of a text for the feminist thinkers of the time, rather as Doris Lessing's *The Golden Notebook* has been since. It was with Lyndall that Roland compared Vera, Lyndall with whom she was to compare herself during coming years. From then on, they wrote to each other.

During the three-day visit of Vera and her mother to Uppingham Prize Day – when Roland won nearly all the prizes in English, Greek and Latin (the classical prizes being the most important in a public school of the time) – the relationship developed. Roland made it happen. Vera was still sentimentally interested in Mr Ward, the vicar, but the two young people had several opportunities to meet and talk, particularly as Roland's parents had been unable to come and see their son leave school carrying many prizes with him. Much of the talk was about Edward. Roland, especially, seemed to think he was letting

Edward down by falling in love with his sister. Vera reports in her diary,

I said goodbye to him with more indifference than I felt. I could not help wondering whether and when I shall see him again. He seems even in a short acquaintance to share both my faults and my talents and my ideas in a way that I have never found anyone else to do.

So by now the prospect of Oxford was enhanced by the thought that if she passed the exam which would give her the final entry qualification, she would go there not only with her brother, but with Roland also. But this was the middle of July, 1914. As in a tragedy, only a little more than a fortnight after the romantic summer days at Uppingham the war began.

At first the war seems to have been more a source of romantic enthusiasm than grim reality for this sheltered and profoundly bored twenty-year-old woman. She records her thoughts for posterity on the day war broke out: 'Today has been too exciting for me to feel at all like sleep – in fact it is one of the most thrilling I have ever lived through.' This is pardonable in a young woman, but it is not so different from how many older, and presumably wiser, people felt. Britain was invincible; the war would be over by Christmas; the nation would have its heroes again. Thomas Brittain, with his aptitude for pessimism, came into his own. Unlike half the country's patriotic parents, he did not want his son to join up. Vera and her mother did. The row went on for weeks. 'Daddy does not care about Edward's honour and courage,' writes Vera passionately, and adds ungrammatically: 'It is left to Edward and I to live up to our name of

"Brittain".' Another entry, in September, begins, 'The morning opened in gloom, owing to Daddy's unconquerable aversion to Edward's doing anything for his country.' Nevertheless, six weeks after the war began Edward left for Oxford, to join up, 'roaring with laughter at Mother's anxiety on his behalf'. He went, like so many, out of patriotism and the desire to serve. It was not until 1917, three and a half million volunteers later, that the flow dried up and the Government had to introduce conscription. By the autumn when she, Edward and Roland should have gone to Oxford together, Vera went there alone. Edward was in the army; Roland, who had previously mentioned his weak eyes as a disqualification, had still not joined. He seems to have written an ambiguous letter, totally lacking in the high sentiments expected of young men at the time. He was writing from a confusing domestic situation where money was short. It is probably true that by that stage all his hopes hinged on getting to Oxford, doing very well and leaving to get some superior position in Government or reputable journalism. Even his career at Oxford may have been in question because of the family finances. Yet in spite of what looks like a shortage of enthusiasm in a former colour sergeant in the Uppingham Officers' Training Corps, he was soon in uniform, with Edward and all their friends from the same year at school. Part of the tragedy of these young men, who were going almost certainly to their deaths, was that they had been reared on the classics, full of the spirit of *dulce et decorum*, the idea that it was beautiful and appropriate to die for your country. They were off to hold the bridge against the Etruscans for Rome, or to die in the pass at Thermopylae; and their mothers, Roman matrons to a woman, were telling them to return on their shields, or with them. The determination to send husbands and sons to war and the hysterical lamentation when they died, not on fields of battle full of waving plumes and clashing shields, but degradingly in the mud of the trenches of France and Belgium, now seems embarrassing. The Roman matrons turned into Dionysiac mourners.

What the men were signing up for – one million in 1914, a second million in 1915 and a third in 1916 – was initially supposed to be a short, sharp war, which would last perhaps six months, followed by an inevitable victory, after which the heroes would come home, proved men. In fact the German advances towards Britain on the one hand and Russia on the other were both stopped, and the British and Russian armies immobilized the Germans on the Western and Eastern fronts. The Germans' effort to reach the coasts of Belgium and France and thus be in a position to invade Britain by sea had been prevented. Both armies dug in across 400 miles of territory, where they lived in trenches opposite each other, with a no man's land of sometimes as little as fifty yards in between them. Thrust and counter-thrust took place. The gains, if there were any, were measured in yards, not miles. It was to this static war, which was to last four years, with its huge casualty list, its terrible living conditions and quickly-buried dead who, in various states of decomposition, surfaced during explosions or bad weather, that the Belgians, the French, the Commonwealth troops and, as from 1918, the American troops were committed. It was for this that Vera's brother, lover and all the others had volunteered.

Nevertheless, by Christmas 1914 neither Edward nor Roland had left the country. The love affair progressed. Vera, down from Oxford after a term and just twenty-one, was invited or organized an invitation to her aunt's house in Putney so that she could go to London, see Roland and meet his mother for the first time. Vera spent an evening with her family and she and Roland met for lunch and went to a play, always accompanied, of course, because it would not have been right for them to have been alone. A group consisting of Vera, her aunt, Roland, Marie Leighton, Roland's mother, and her daughter Clare, then sixteen, also had tea in a hotel. Vera was very nervous about the encounter, since this, as far as she was concerned, was the first meeting with her future husband's family, although it is very unlikely that Marie Leighton – a flamboyant figure in a velvet coat trimmed with fur, a feathered hat and a low-necked blouse – saw the tea party in this light. At one point Mrs Leighton said, 'I am *so* glad I was able to meet you. I wanted so much to see Edward's sister,' to which Vera protested, perhaps rather gauchely, 'Oh, only for that reason?'

It was the visit to London which seems to have confirmed the feelings of both the young people. They were never alone but during one revealing conversation when they were walking along Vera remarked that she wanted to see the play based on *David Copperfield* because the character of Steerforth had always appealed to her. Roland replied that Steerforth was the finest character in the book. The exchange looks like a coded message – Steerforth is not, after all, the finest character in the book. He is a minor character, the villain who seduces and ruins little Em'ly, who has been brought up as a sister to his friend David Copperfield. The analogy is fairly plain. Edward is the doughty David Copperfield, Roland is Steerforth and Vera is the sister, Em'ly. In this conversation Vera and Roland actually acknowledge all this and Vera in a sense assents to her own seduction, which never took place.

Eventually they found themselves, with Vera's aunt in attendance, of course, at the station waiting for Vera's train. Nothing was said between them, nor could be, but Vera records that in the train she thought, 'I would give all I had lived or hoped for during the brief years of my existence, not to astonish the world by some brief and glittering achievement, but some day to be the mother of Roland Leighton's child.' She was completely in love, wholly committed.

In some ways Roland Leighton was not an ordinary public schoolboy of the time and had not behaved like one. He had courted Vera, his friend's big sister, discreetly but assiduously, since his school days. There was no way in which he could make her an offer of marriage. He had not even been to university, let alone begun to earn a living, and there was no money on his side to keep them. It must be remembered that the kind of attention he was paying her might easily have been expected, in those days, to lead to a proposal of marriage. Vera, for her part, could not go very far in encouraging this attention without looking too keen, and, if the proposal did not come, slightly tarnishing her own reputation. Yet she, who had just started what was meant to be a three-year course at university, was taking him seriously enough to go to London to meet not only him but his mother. No one can know what was said between mother and son when it appeared he was courting Vera seriously.

When the time came for Vera to go back to Oxford again a fortnight later, she managed to meet Roland in Leicester *en route* without her parents' knowledge, carefully re-arranging the times so that they would not find out. After a journey spent in semi-silence he kissed her hand, she was too shy to respond, and then, at Oxford, she got off the train. It all seems extremely quaint but we are dealing with a carefully reared middle-class girl and a young man brought up to respect women. The message was plain none the less. He desperately wanted to see her and she had taken illicit steps to meet him. In her later account Vera records a con-versation about going to Florence with Roland, hinting at marriage, perhaps a honeymoon, but this story does not appear in her diary.

By March, after Vera had come back from Oxford, Roland was visiting the family at Buxton. This time there was a long talk after dinner in private between Roland and Thomas Brittain. Then she and Roland were left alone by the drawing room fire – Roland had evidently convinced her father that he was not Steerforth; Thomas Brittain had warned him he had better not be. A courtship, of a mild kind, was being permitted. He sat near her but there was no lovemaking, nor could there be. He could not propose mar-riage, since he was, as Vera says, 'so young and poor', and because he could not make this offer he could not make love to her. There was no honourable way forward. And he was about to be posted to France where he might be killed.

Who was this young man, who had managed to captivate the intelligent and romantic young Vera? She was certainly sensitive about his appearance and records her mother, her aunt and a nurse at the hospital where she worked all saying at different times that he was not plain, perhaps something of an indication that he was. Certainly his appearance was not in the style of the times, which demanded of men that they should be tall and fair with clean-cut features and blue eyes – the poet Rupert Brooke was the ideal. Roland, not particularly tall, had heavy black eyebrows and full lips. His looks were more of the kind a romantic novelist might call 'smouldering' – he might be considered much handsomer today. There is a photograph of him taken in the uniform of the Officers' Training Corps at Uppingham, with Edward Brittain and another friend, Victor Richardson. Edward sits, smiling mildly, slightly aside from the other two, legs apart, relaxed. The small features which made Vera into a pretty girl turn him into a mild, pleasant-faced but unemphatic-looking young man. Victor Richardson, leaning against Roland Leighton as they share a seat on what looks like a tea chest, is round-faced, more boyish than the other two. Roland is in the middle. His uniform jacket is open, revealing his open-necked shirt (the others are buttoned up to the chin). He looks uncertain but determined, and actually, compared with the others, a little thuggish. It is he who draws the eye. The other two look predictable: one can easily see Edward, the musician, as the future humane and intelligent senior bureaucrat drawing up plans for prison reform or the governing of some huge tract of Empire on the other side of the world. One can see

Victor as the competent but not very energetic manager of a bank or partner in a respectable firm of lawyers. But Roland, quite angry-looking, with something of a Brando-esque sulk, looks more a force to be reckoned with. In the photograph he sent to Vera in 1914 he is pictured in Army uniform, but again he gives the impression of being older than his years and rather fierce. Of course, the possession of heavy black brows, deep-set black eyes fringed with sooty lashes and a heavy mouth tend not to impart an inoffensive air. And each generation has its 'photograph face'. At that time a photograph was considered to be in the nature of a portrait: womanly calm and a rather spiritual expression was standard for women, an air of manly assurance for men. Perhaps Roland was getting his expression wrong through a combination of youth and embarrassment (and, in the case of the Army photograph, fear). Yet, unless the two photographs utterly belie him, his roughness, determination and egotism are disconcerting. You begin to wonder whether the marriage of two such passionate characters would really have worked. Would Roland have turned into the steady family man required in those days of uncertain contraception and little employment for women, when a wife and a family needed the greatest protection a man could supply? Similarly, could Vera really have subdued herself sufficiently to the owner of this challenging, demanding face?

It was probably Roland Leighton's background which produced someone who looked rather older and more experienced than the average public schoolboy of his day. Vera is slightly evasive in her treatment of his family situation in *Testament of Youth.* She may have wished not to upset the Leightons and certainly she needed their co-operation over the reproduction of letters and Roland's poems.

When Vera met her, Marie Leighton, known professionally as Marie Connor Leighton, had been supporting throughout her marriage a large ménage, including her husband and three children. Robert Leighton, obviously a pleasant man, was extremely deaf. He made his living by writing stories for boys but was far less successful than his wife. Marie Leighton had published the first of her novels, which eventually totalled sixty-five, when she was only sixteen. She had married at seventeen. Roland, the oldest child of the three, was specially prized when he was born, an earlier child having been allowed to die by a careless servant. He was always her favourite child. By the time Vera entered the scene Marie Leighton was still writing serials in instalments for newspapers, sometimes more than one at a time, but the prosperous days were over and a move from London to Lowestoft, where Vera first found them, had been conducted not long before because funds were running out.

Roland had grown up in London, in St John's Wood, where extravagant living was the order of the day – there were velvet suits for him, the only one of her children, his mother declared, who was worth dressing well; there were silks and laces and jewellery for her; there was a choice every day of four desserts at dinner, and eight on Sundays.

The children led a semi-conventional life, in the charge of a Baptist nanny, who scared them with tales of hell-fire (but this was not unusual), peering intermittently over the bannisters to study the string of almost undoubtedly platonic suitors their mother kept in tow. There was a fat, married judge who called Marie Leighton 'beloved beauty'; a retired naval surgeon, who wore a kilt, had knobbly knees and a St Bernard dog; and a portly bank manager. She also had her brother-in-law, who had fallen in love with her, in a maddened condition. For these details and many more we have her daughter Clare, known to the family as 'the by-stander', to thank. Clare's biography of her mother (*Tempestuous Petticoat*, Gollancz, 1948) ends in 1920 and is a picture mostly of the Leightons' childhood, which had its eccentric side, supervised by this very busy mother and the father who was completely deaf.

Mrs Leighton supported the family more or less single-handed on the proceeds from the novels she wrote – highly sensational works with titles like *The Harvest of Sin*, *The Fires of Love*, *In the Grip of a Life*, *The Heart's Awakening*. They were stories dealing with fires, bankruptcies, false accusations, missing children, imprisonments, innocent maidens, sneering peers, alarming reappearances, kidnappings – the *Dallas* and *Dynasty* of their day. Clare Leighton remembers being on the landing with the other children, very hungry, while the messenger from the *Daily Mail* waited in the hall, his cab outside; no one could have their lunch until her mother had completed the next thrilling instalment to be immediately rushed to the printer. These were children who, unlike their peer group, gleaned their information about sex not from the family medical book but from a book on forensic medicine used by their mother for her sensational novels. This, Clare Leighton reports, gave them a rather peculiar notion of relations between the sexes. As they left for their holidays, with the dogs, the servants and the mounds of luggage, from the hall they could still hear her dictating the last chapter of her latest epic: 'Oh my heart's darling, my own, my joy. Give me one chance to prove my love. Give me time to earn your kisses. Let me woo you and you shall know the happiness of living in the shelter of a good man's love.'

It was a house where everyone worked the whole time except on Christmas Day. As long as the pace could be maintained the household would go on functioning. Unfortunately a quarrel with the proprietor of the *Daily Mail* took place and Marie Leighton's income was reduced. They packed in 1914 and moved to the house at Lowestoft where, as Clare Leighton says, they never quite unpacked. 'It was,' she writes, 'the kind of mansion one might think up in a nightmare. Its name was Heather Cliff and it stood alone on a bluff overlooking the North Sea.' This was where Vera first met the whole family together. Another employer was found but the lengthening casualty lists in the papers and, perhaps, the public's declining taste for Marie Leighton's kind of fiction meant that things were never to be the same again. The following year they were in a cottage in Sussex. This move, said to be away from the bombs, left unpaid servants and bills behind. The bubble had burst. Roland's mother was a strong-hearted woman, supporting her family at a time when women (unless they were brave widows, of course) were not much respected for doing this. Even if her books had been more reputable than they were, there was still something rather dubious about a woman of her class earning a living. It was a woman's job to find a man to support her and then make him happy and comfortable. Women who did not find husbands were, at best, to be pitied, at worst, mocked. Women whose husbands failed to support them had made a mistake in picking the wrong man. Women who worked became 'unfeminine' and 'unattractive': paid employment mysteriously de-sexed them. This may have been part of the reason for Marie Leighton's flamboyant clothes and emotional and romantic manner. She was emphatically feminine.

One day she was denouncing Beethoven, Brahms, Mozart and Bach (on the grounds that of all the great composers only Chopin was capable of loving a woman) and told her daughter that she (Clare) had no conception of passion and romance, her cold Leighton blood being responsible. Clare Leighton says, 'Unknown to her, at that moment Roland was entranced with Gregorian chant, which she must have considered even worse than Beethoven. But as he continued to spend his pocket money on buying her scarlet silk stockings she had no notion of his heresies.' Certainly she demanded a high level of courtship behaviour from her oldest son. This kind of extravagant language and lover-like behaviour between mother and son was not unusual at the time. 'He has been my Prince,' Marie Leighton said to Vera, 'and I've always worshipped and adored him so.'

There were reasons for this style – on the mother's side sons were all-important and might become more so as she grew older. In moneyed families when the father died all the property would go to the first son, who would then become responsible for the whole family and more or less absolutely for his mother. Sons were not just a woman's status, but often, later, her fate. In a society where divorce was uncommon, too, some of the love a woman might have felt for her husband could be transferred to the son, although this does not seem to have been the case with the Leightons. Marie Leighton insisted on male devotion from many quarters ('Mother's old men' and 'the also-rans' was how Roland divided her suitors up). Her son was only one among many devoted lovers. Roland seems to have gone along with the system without really believing in it. In a household full of dogs, huge rolled-up sheets of paper containing the plots for his mother's sensational novels, messengers in the hall and constant extravagance of feeling (Mrs Leighton spoke like the characters in her novels) her intelligent children seem to have maintained a friendly but determined attitude to life. They had a lot of practice in hanging on to reality, since their mother's life, and her work, ignored it. They had a much larger range of experience than their contemporaries; they went their own way; and Roland, especially, seems to have met his mother's need for glamour, emotion and attention while largely keeping his real thoughts to himself. It must have been an embarrassing background from which to come – few of the boys at Uppingham can have had their fees paid by their mother's bad novels. It was also an insecure background, compared with what the others might expect in the way of inherited money, family firms to go into or influential friends. But it accounts for much in his relationship with Vera. He had all the confidence of someone who has held his course in an erratic home and he was certainly not short of experience in pleasing women. He slowly but surely changed the course of Vera's life.

What this young man became in the end was part of the national myth of the dead of the First World War; a myth so powerful it seems to go back to that of the young, dying god, and certainly to the story of Christ, though without the hope of renewal and salvation. In March 1915 he was posted abroad. In April he was in the trenches and Vera's next term at Oxford was spent agonizing over the casualty lists and waiting for his letters. By June she could stand it no longer and had characteristically decided to take action, do the end-of-year examinations, then leave to start nursing. At the end of June she was back in Buxton working as an auxiliary at the Devonshire Hospital, a convalescent hospital for soldiers. The work mainly consisted of cleaning, preparing or serving meals and, at first, probably for reasons of propriety, taking care of the extremities – fingers and toes only – of the wounded. Gradually, however, she was given more responsibility and her attitude to the work becomes more sober – one man was to be lame for ever, another died. She was, of course, still always waiting for a letter from Roland.

When he came back to England in August she met him in London and they agreed, on the train to Buxton, that they might marry. However, they left Buxton without informing the Brittains positively that they had this in mind. 'She says she can't make up her mind, the little fool,' Vera overheard her mother telling her father in the bathroom. 'That's just like Vera. You never know where you are with her.' During a stay with the Leightons at the house on the cliff at Lowestoft they revealed to the perhaps astounded Mrs Leighton that they would marry in three years or after the war. The scruples which had seemed important the previous year must have seemed less so for both, after Roland's months in France. In London, before Roland's return to the front, she says in her diary that he bought a wicked-looking knife, which he played with nervously over tea with the family. In *Testament of Youth* she says he stocked up with morphine. Whether he did one or both of these things, it indicates something of what Roland expected on his return to the front. The thought horrified him. At least when he left England he had the comfort of being engaged, and back in France he also became a Roman Catholic. It is as if he needed the comfort of a future in this world and also beyond it. He was twenty years old.

Presumably, also, the kind of objections the two sets of parents might have presented before the war changed everything were less likely to be made. When told of the engagement after Roland had left for France, Thomas Brittain – who, after all, had not been consulted – merely said the idea was ridiculous, since Roland was going to be killed anyway. Edith Brittain was probably more sympathetic. She came from a family with no business or capital and so would have been more receptive to Roland's having to work for a living, and she must have seen that Vera was in love, something which might appeal more to a mother than to the prospective father-in-law of a penniless soldier in uniform. At any rate the engagement, by that stage, was only what used to be called 'unofficial'; an official engagement was more binding and more public, involving announcements in newspapers, engagement parties attended by both sides of the family, detailed plans about accommodation and money and, usually, the fixing of an actual date for the wedding.

Thomas and Edith Brittain had effectively lost control of Vera, as they must have been beginning to realize. She had already gone to Oxford and had become engaged. Now she applied for a post as a VAD (volunteer nurse) in London, was accepted and went. It is very doubtful whether she would have been able to live away from home in a large city without opposition had there been no war, although, as it happened, the family soon followed on her heels. Thomas Brittain retired from the family business, and although a relatively young man, was never to work again. (He died in 1935.) Thomas and Edith Brittain moved first to Brighton and then to a flat in Kensington.

From October 1915 Vera was at the First London General Hospital in Camberwell, living in a chilly cubicle in a house a mile and a half from the hospital, a distance which she and the other nurses often had to walk, or run, in all weathers, if the trams were full. Her hours were from 7.30 in the morning to 8 at night, with three hours off in the middle of the day and half a day off a week, although this off-duty time went by the board after big offensives, when huge convoys of wounded would come in from the front. This was no convalescent hospital; it was the place which received seriously injured men – those who had survived the dressing stations to which they were taken straight after the battle, the hospitals further away from the battle lines, and then the long boat and train journey home. The sights, sounds and indeed smells were terrible. Vera reports that the soldiers played gramophone records all the time in the wards, which covered the sound of those groaning in pain.

There was a row with Roland over letters. She had reproached him with writing too seldom; he became angry about what must have looked like terrible ignorance of how he was actually living. But the letters began again. In December he wrote to say he had leave in the New Year. Then it was cancelled, then the dates were changed again, and on Christmas morning she left for Brighton, where she waited in her hotel all day for a message to say that Roland had arrived. At the cottage in Keymer, seven miles away, to which the family had moved, the Leightons sat up until after midnight over dinner, waiting for Roland. On Boxing Day, according to *Testament of Youth* (the day after, according to her diary), she was called to the telephone in the morning. Of course she thought it was the news of Roland's arrival. But at this moment of hope, when Vera was even thinking of an early, immediate marriage, the news was cruel. The caller was Roland's sister Clare, saying that he was dead. He had gone out to check the barbed wire defences in front of the entrenchments on the night of the 23rd, in moonlight, had been shot in the stomach, carried back and – let us hope they told Vera the truth about this – been given enough morphia to knock him out until next day, when he was operated on at the clearing station ten miles away and died. He was just one of the 300,000 dead, out of the two and a half million men who had already joined up. The final death toll would be a million; the French and Germans lost twice as many.

For Vera this was probably the saddest time of her life. Later she was to have her share of grief and anxiety, but here she faced the loss of a lover, and a future, a day before her own twenty-second birthday, with no previous experience of loss to sustain her. The final horror, that she was expecting news of a joyful meeting and instead heard Roland was dead, can only have made the immediate shock worse.

She spent the week with the Leightons at Keymer, then returned to the hospital at Camberwell to continue nursing. That this was now a sacrificial act is marked, perhaps, by the way she begins to use capital letters for the words 'He' and 'Him' when referring to Roland in her diary, as if he were Jesus Christ. 'Wandered about Camberwell alone, extremely miserable,' reads one entry. Her position could hardly have been worse – she was young, facing acute grief, working among the survivors, who were a perpetual reminder of Roland's death, the war was only eighteen months old and public acceptance of constant bereavement and how to treat the bereaved was not established. The streets were not yet, as they would be, full of people wearing mourning. She had not even been, after all, the official fiancée of the dead man. There would be no funeral, where grief could be released and the body laid to rest. One of the agonies of the time was that there was so seldom a corpse: a man went out in full health and a telegram came back saying he was dead, leaving the bereaved to dwell on how the man had died, where and how he had been buried.

In her grief Vera turned to those who should have been able to share it with her. Whether the Leightons were much support is a different matter. Not only had Roland, the idol of the household, been killed, but times were hard. The cottage was kept going by one gypsy daily-woman. Marie Leighton and her daughter had to cook – neither had ever learned how – and Marie Leighton, even without the loss of her favourite son, could never have dealt with reduced circumstances in the approved way. She seems to have done her best to console Vera, but it must have been difficult to sustain the proprieties of mourning between mother and intended wife while facing so many problems.

It was late January, Vera records in *Testament of Youth*, when she made her way through muddy lanes back to the station after a dreadful visit to the Leightons. She had arrived that morning, she says, to discover Marie Leighton and her daughter standing in a room with Roland's returned kit, including his bullet-holed tunic and blood-stained vest. The terrible smell of mud and blood coming from the kit caused Marie Leighton to turn to her husband and appeal to him to take the clothes away and burn or bury them. 'They are not Roland; they even seem to detract from his memory and spoil his glamour. I won't have anything more to do with them!' she is said to have declared.

It was, indeed, common practice to send the dead soldier's effects back to his family. What is curious about this incident is that the diary entry by Vera, found detached from the main body of her journal, is dated January 13, not the end of January as she says in *Testament of Youth*. In her Introduction to Vera's complete journal, published in 1981, Clare Leighton, in 1980, recalls a totally different story. She remembers, as a girl of sixteen, following her father down the garden carrying two kettles of boiling water. Keeping an eye on the windows behind them to make sure his wife was not watching, he carried Roland's blood-stained tunic. He had sneaked the horrible garment out of Roland's effects after they were delivered, before Marie Leighton could see it. Clare's task was to throw the boiling water on the frozen earth so that her father could dig a hole and bury the tunic surreptitiously. Thus according to Vera's 'official' account in *Testament of Youth*, all the kit, including the tunic, was on the floor and it was the end of January, when there were puddles in the lane to the station; her diary gives us much the same account but is dated mid-January; Clare Leighton's account gives no date, but certainly mentions a very cold day, when the ground was solidly frozen, and says the tunic was secretly buried by herself and Richard Leighton. Also missing, obviously, is Mrs Leighton's emotional speech to her husband appealing to him to dispose of the tunic. Marie Leighton was indeed capable of this, but it is not likely, given that Robert Leighton was deaf. Admittedly Clare Leighton's account was written when she was over eighty, sixty-five years after the event, but the story is very clear, and it is not a scene one would be likely to invent. Nowhere in Clare's account is Vera mentioned. Even stranger is the fact that in Clare Leighton's biography of her mother, written in 1948, she recalls the arrival of Roland's kit, though in less detail, and again does not mention Vera as having been there. However, this is perhaps not such a great surprise since throughout the book she never mentions Vera at all.

One explanation for these discrepancies is that Clare

Leighton simply forgot what happened, although there is something horribly plausible about having to throw hot water on the ground so that your father could dig a hole for your dead brother's blood-stained tunic. Another possibility is that, although Vera Brittain said she was there at the time, she was not. She needed to be there, with the mother and sister of the dead hero as they gazed on his blood-stained clothing, the trio of womenfolk going through a catharsis of mourning. There would, after all, be no funeral. The only detail which convinces one that she was there is the horror of the dank-smelling uniform: 'All the sepulchres and catacombs of Rome could not make me realise mortality and decay and corruption as vividly as did the smell of those clothes,' she writes, and this carries, somehow, the ring of truth. All we can say is that we may never quite know what happened or who was there on that day when all that was left of Roland Leighton went back to his family.

Aside from that it might well be that she found only limited consolation at the Leightons'. Her own parents showed their normal kindness, advised her to have a break from the hospital, gave her money, but possibly they had always seen Vera's love affair as an over-hasty matter, precipitated by the war. In any case they must have been more worried about their son, now in France himself. Really, no one could help. Vera plodded on at the hospital. She never got what she wanted in the way of proper mourning (she was to be insistent on forms of mourning, proper flowers, ceremonies and memorials all her life). This lack of help or release must have contributed to her state of near-collapse when the war ended.

'I had bitterness enough in my nature before,' she writes in her diary. 'I didn't need suffering to soften me, I needed joy ... Nothing matters. I can't make it matter.' Now she put her name down for foreign service, knowing that it might mean being sent to Malta, Egypt, Salonika or France. In the end she was picked for Malta.

Before she left, her brother had arrived at the hospital, wounded in the arm and leg in the first day of the battle of the Somme. The British Army was ordered to walk, not run, towards enemy lines which ought to have been knocked out by a week's heavy bombardment. The German lines, even the German barbed wire, turned out to be largely intact and on 1 July 1916, the first day of what would be months of battle, 60,000 British soldiers were killed. It is a day which now sums up the mixture of courage and trust among the soldiers and the monumental stupidity of the Chiefs of Staff; at the time it provided yet another clue for a still largely unsuspecting public to what the war was really like.

Edward, already wounded in the leg and unable to move, had been hit in the arm while hiding in a foxhole. He had finally crawled seventy yards through dead, decomposing and dying men, back to the British lines, where he got a stretcher party sent out to collect the other wounded man in the foxhole. A third was all right, but simply refused to go out and fight. Edward was awarded the Military Cross, not for this, but for getting his men to attack in the first place. After watching the first wave of men being scythed down, at walking pace, by enemy machine gun fire, subsequent battalions were ordered to advance over the top. Edward Brittain's men, the 2nd Sherwood Foresters, formed their

Above: (l. to r.) Thomas Brittain, Vera, Edward and Edith

Right: Vera and Edward (*c.* 1897)

Above: Vera at Melrose, Buxton
(*c.* 1913)

Left: Vera at Melrose, Buxton
(*c.* 1913)

The Uppingham friends: Victor Richardson, Roland Leighton and
Edward Brittain. Uppingham Officers' Training Corps (July 1914)

The portrait Roland sent Vera in
December 1914

The portrait Vera sent Roland
Leighton in December 1914

Vera, in pyjamas, when a VAD in Malta (1916)

Vera in VAD uniform, Malta (1916)

Vera and some of her patients at St George's Hospital, Malta (1916)

Wounded soldiers in France, waiting for transport to a base hospital
similar to the one at Etaples (1916)

Winifred Holtby at Brigne (1921)

Wedding of Vera Brittain and George Catlin: (l. to r.) Edith Brittain, the Rev. George Catlin (George's father), George Catlin, Vera Brittain, Thomas Brittain, Winifred Holtby (1925)

Vera with John and Shirley (*c.* 1932)

Winifred Holtby (early
1930s)

Vera Brittain, aged forty-
three (1936)

Vera at Winifred's grave
(1954)

Vera and George (1954)

own opinion of the situation and had to be forced at gunpoint by Edward Brittain – doing his duty bravely, although there must have been many families in Nottingham afterwards wishing he had been less conscientious. It was not unusual for officers to have to get their men out of the trenches at gunpoint. It was in order for an officer to shoot a soldier on the spot for cowardice. It was not all that unusual for the men to shoot an over-zealous officer; the casualty rate generally among the officers being much higher, they were frequently novices and less experienced than the men they led. Of course, it was more dangerous for a man to shoot an officer than vice versa, since he would be court-martialled if found out. The mutual violence was an inevitable result of trench warfare, intolerable conditions and nerves stretched by perpetual bombardment and fear. Robert Graves was heavily criticized over ten years later for saying in his war memoirs that after surviving a few years in the trenches a great many officers became alcoholics.

Vera, though thrilled by Edward's decoration for bravery, was, perhaps, less than generous about it. She was jealous for Roland. 'How could he have endured, the next autumn term, to be a silent witness of Edward's clamorous reception at Uppingham? – a reception such as we had often imagined for himself but had never even have thought possible for Edward, except perhaps years and years later as a great violinist and composer,' she wrote.

Before Edward had left England after recovering from his wounds Vera was on her way to Malta to nurse. Ships were being torpedoed and she was frightened. Nevertheless she saw, for the first time, the Mediterranean, the Aegean,

Greece. More than safety, perhaps, she needed a break from the horrors of wartime nursing, hard living conditions and neglected grief. She was always, although she may not then have known it, someone who benefited from travel and could lose some of her cares once she was on the move. The months of nursing convalescent troops, far from home, may have helped her but could not, of course, remove the pain of Roland's loss, nor her anxieties for Edward, now back in France.

The coming of spring in Malta might have made a difference (she disliked the cold and always found winter a trial) had the news not arrived in April that Victor Richardson, the third young man in the Uppingham picture showing Roland and Edward, had been blinded at Arras, leading his platoon into battle. A fortnight later she heard that Geoffrey Thurlow, another great Uppingham friend, had been killed. 'Time to take a long, long adieu,' Victor had told her he had written to Edward. The young men who had gone from school to the trenches were now under no illusions about their chances of survival. Vera, knowing Victor was in England, blinded and therefore at least safe from going back to France, made what seems an odd decision: she would go home and marry him. Her motives must have been mixed. She wanted to help him; she wanted to dedicate herself to one of the wounded. Roland was dead; perhaps Victor seemed a replacement. What is more, by that time there seemed to be no reason why every man in the country of fighting age should not be killed or wounded. There would be no one to marry after the war. It may have been a mercy for her that she was never able to implement this decision, taken too soon after bereavement. She began to visit Victor in hospital as soon as she arrived in England, in May. Sadly, ten days after her arrival, he died.

By August 1916 she was at the hospital at Etaples, in Normandy. She slept in a wooden hut, through the window of which snow fell on her bed in winter. France was the apotheosis of her wartime experience. She had been moving, from the beginning of the war, closer and closer to the centre of the action. Now she was there – the Etaples hospital was only about forty miles from the British lines. Bombardments could be heard from there, the wounded came in lorries direct from the dressing stations and although at the time there was no immediate physical danger – there was an agreement hospitals should not be shelled – a German breakthrough would have meant sudden evacuation or capture. In fact after Vera left, the hospital was actually bombed by the Germans during raids on a nearby railway depot.

At first she was assigned to nursing the German casualties, then, throughout the long, cold winter, she worked on the medical wards for British troops – stoking the stoves, carrying bedpans, taking temperatures and pulses, washing the patients, giving out medicines. There were blistered, suffocating victims of mustard gas, men suffering from fevers of every kind, pneumonia and T B. In the spring the Germans began a big offensive, one great push designed to break through the British lines, reach the Channel ports and finally put them in a position to invade Britain. Vera's ward was converted to a surgical ward. For a month the casualties turned up in ambulances, lorries and cattle trucks. The

VADs, who were not supposed to be any more than nurses' assistants, except in grave emergencies, were fully employed. Vera describes herself on one occasion, alone in the ward,

gazing half-hypnotised at the dishevelled beds, the stretchers on the floor, the scattered boots and piles of muddy khaki, the brown blankets turned back from smashed limbs bound to splints by filthy blood-stained bandages. Beneath each stinking wad of sodden wool and gauze an obscene horror waited for me – and all the equipment I had for attacking it in this ex-medical ward was one pair of forceps standing in a potted-meat glass half-full of methylated spirit.

As the Germans came closer and bombs began to fall near by Vera's father wrote to say that her mother was ill. Because of the difficulty of getting servants – women had found better-paid work in factories or were doing men's work of all kinds – Edith Brittain could not be cared for at home and so had gone into a nursing home to be looked after, while Thomas Brittain, lacking her care, had moved into an hotel. They needed Vera to return and look after them. That they called her back from nursing dying soldiers to take care of them was not at all surprising. Both Vera and, even more, Winifred Holtby, were to find over the years, as they were appealed to from one family sick-bed after another, that no matter what other obligations a single daughter might have, family claims had to be considered paramount. It may also be that the Brittains, apart from being worn down by wartime difficulties they could not cope with, were gravely afraid for Vera as the Germans advanced. Edward was now in Italy, where his chances of surviving might have been considered slightly higher, but now Vera was in France, in danger.

She had to break her contract when she left France in 1918 and went back to Britain. Her mother's illness turned out to be nothing serious and she spent the next few months taking care of things in a London flat, afflicted by careless or non-existent servants. It is a curious thing that this woman, whose resolution stopped at virtually nothing, who was not deterred by a gangrenous leg or torpedoes, who would go on to rear her children more or less single-handed while keeping a large house running by her own efforts, was nevertheless always thrown out by the lack of servants, inadequate servants or servants falling ill. The only thing she felt unable to do was what nearly every other woman in the world takes for granted: physically run her own household.

It was a grim time. Vera was exhausted. The final blow came when, after reports that the Austrians were mounting a big offensive in Italy, the news arrived of Edward's death. He had survived eighteen months as a junior officer in the trenches and a further six months in Italy. During all that time he seems to have been unflinchingly brave, he never lost his morale and he wrote to Vera with unstinting patience after the loss of Roland, no matter what conditions he was enduring himself. The authorities had initially kept him hanging about in England for a long time before posting him abroad, perhaps because they considered him unpromising officer material; in the event he seems to have reacted as well as any and probably better than most.

Vera, nursing, rather dully, in London and already

suffering from the low-grade depression which was to afflict her for many years to come, did not celebrate Edward's death in reams of prose, as she had Roland's. She did not search out brother officers who might have been there when he died nor enquire anxiously into every detail of his death, as she had with Roland. She was too tired properly to register this last blow, which she had been dreading for so long. Fifteen years later, though, after she had written, dry-eyed, the earlier parts of *Testament of Youth*, including the portions about Roland's death, she found herself weeping as she wrote about Edward's. She says she had to take off her reading glasses, as they were so misty and, character-istically, go on writing without them.

Five months after Edward was killed the war ended. After Vera's nursing contract expired and during the months of waiting to return to Oxford she appears to have been like someone going through a fog, one of the walking wounded of the war. Apart from the depression caused by too much stress and pain, like so many of the survivors she had to endure a kind of acute loneliness. Those who had not been to war had no conception of what it had been like. Nothing in their lives gave them any clue. This had been the first time for a century that Britain had faced a foe equal in terms of power and strength. It was the first time any nation had fought a mechanized war, which had become in-creasingly technological as the battle went on – machine-guns, tanks and mustard gas had all been used for the first time. Television, of course, did not exist (if it had, the war might well have ended in 1916). The only information came through newspapers and unsophisticated war photography.

It was not merely a question of not being able to imagine what had happened; it was not being able to accept that patriotism had been betrayed, courage wasted and heroism pointless. The inhabitants of a country with such a long history of victory and conquest lacked the vocabulary to express what had happened, particularly when they were mourning a million dead. It was like the reaction of America after the Vietnam War. For Vera, and the others, there was an enormous gulf between the experience, even the ways of thought, of those who had been to war and those who had not.

Aside from the immediate lack of communication with her contemporaries and the near breakdown caused by strain and grief, she faced a future with little prospect of marriage. 'It's one's future, not one's past, that they really hide, those graves in France,' says one of the young women in Vera's first novel, *The Dark Tide*, written in 1922. By 1919, when she went back to Somerville, she was approaching twenty-six years old, which was quite old for marriage by the standards of the time. 'A generation gone,' went the litany of the time, which was not literally true, but was much more true of the middle and upper classes who wrote the litanies. They had sustained the heaviest casualties among their sons, who tended to have had some prior form of military training – almost all the better schools had an Officers' Training Corps – and who were in any case automatically made officers on a class basis. Men like Siegfried Sassoon who volunteered as private soldiers were subjected to pressure to become officers. And the junior officers, because they had to lead and be seen to be leading, were six times as likely to be killed as their men. Moreover they had been brought up to believe that if they had privileges, they also had responsibilities. When a crisis came they had to be better than the rest. The less-privileged were less embarrassed about looking after their own skins. My own childhood, among men whose only First World War medals were awarded for long service, rang with the phrases, 'Never volunteer,' and 'Better a live coward than a dead hero,' but such are the sentiments of those not reared from childhood to set a good example. The young men Vera would have married were exactly those killed in the greatest numbers.

Another reason was that at the beginning of the war over 40 per cent of possible recruits were refused by army doctors as being too sickly, or just too small, to join the army. The height requirement, originally 5′ 8″, had to be reduced to 5′ 3″. Even then the army had to form the 'bantam brigades' of men who, though fit, did not meet the height requirement. The average height of 16,000 young men examined during recruitment in the West Midlands was only 5′ 5½″, and a similar group of Liverpudlians had an *average* chest measurement of 31″. Since full kit, in which a soldier might be required to march fifteen miles, or run, weighed 60 pounds, there was obviously no point in recruiting men who were about the size of today's eleven-year-olds. TB and chronic bronchitis were among the main illnesses found at recruiting stations. Poverty and poor living conditions, especially in the industrial cities of the North Midlands and Scotland, were mainly responsible for the small stature and bad health of the potential soldiers. All this plainly threw the burden of the struggle on the better nourished and better-off – thus the 'missing generation' consisted of the healthiest and strongest, leaving the nation with the permanent impression that the best had been taken and the worst left behind to run the country after the war. Whether myth or fact, this thought coloured the views of the survivors and provided an explanation for a future which turned out worse than anticipated.

The 'missing generation' did not, obviously, include women, and this is the point at which the term 'surplus women' came into the language, words which still make me, two generations later, feel very uneasy. Men now vastly outnumber women in Britain but no one describes them as 'surplus men' nor ever will. It sums up all the dread women felt, even a generation later, about the women who had never married and were 'left on the shelf'. There were very few ways for a woman to keep herself, still less achieve any status or dignity, outside marriage. A second cliché, where basic Freudian tenets hit street level, so to speak, was applied to such unmarried women: they were 'frustrated spinsters', women who, in spite of all appearances to the contrary, might be mad, or about to go mad at any moment, for want of sex or children. It is as if the old notion that unmarried women were failures had not changed but had merely been brought up to date by Freud. Remaining unmarried could not now be treated as a personal failure but it could be suggested that lack of sexual and maternal fulfilment could turn unmarried women into little better than lunatics. The reason may well be that for the four years of the war women, married and single, childless and mothers, had been doing men's work. There had to be a reason why women, and particularly the women most willing and available for work, were not really qualified to do it. The 'frustrated spinster' argument was the answer. As Winifred Holtby, a lifelong spinster, wrote acutely at the time,

When I was a child an unmarried woman who had compromised her reputation for strict chastity was an outcast; she was called fallen, unfortunate or wicked, according to the degree of charity in those who mentioned her. Today there is a far worse crime than promiscuity: it is chastity.

On the other hand, Vera had some faith in the theory that marriage was essential and celibacy highly deleterious to women. She reduced Phyllis Bentley, the novelist (an unmarried woman), to tears on the subject. Meanwhile, the spinsters of the First World War capably took over jobs in schools, hospitals, the Civil Service and elsewhere, but it continued to be maintained that single women in jobs had something subtly wrong with them; any mistakes, or nastiness, were due to their mental condition; they could crack at any moment.

In spite of her depression and her conviction that she would never marry, Vera's efforts before the war had at least given her some immediate purpose and some future hope. She published her *Verses of a VAD* before going back to Oxford. They attracted no attention, which was perhaps a blessing in disguise, since most of the poems are extremely banal. In only one does stale poetic language not scupper the thought and the rhythm follow the sense of what is being said. It certainly expresses what she must have felt at the time:

I am so tired.
The dying sun incarnadines the West,
And every shadow with its gold is fired;
And all I loved the best
Is gone and every good that I desired
Passes away, an idle hopeless quest;
Even the Highest, whereto I aspired,
Has vanished with the rest.
I am so tired.

At Oxford, 'in a chill room at whose door nobody knocked', she continued to work for her history degree – after what had happened she changed her degree course from English to history. Another person might have sunk completely beneath the weight of her depression. She suffered from the obsession that her face was altering, sometimes becoming like a witch's, sometimes growing a beard. At a college debate where she supported the motion 'that four years' travel are better education than four years at University,' she spoke of the war and plainly upset the other students, all of whom were younger and nearly all without her experience. She was trounced by a good-humoured speech by a fellow student on the other side. She rushed back, humiliated and despairing, to her lodgings where she fell on the floor, crying.

It was not as if the attack, as she construed it, came from a stranger. She had been sharing tutorials in modern European history with the other young woman since the previous year. It was not as if that woman spoke in ignorance. She herself, unlike most of the other undergraduates, had been involved in the war. First she had been a probationer nurse at a London nursing home, helping to fill the gap in civilian nursing left as the qualified staff withdrew to nurse the troops; after a year at Oxford she left, just as Vera had, because she could not tolerate student life while the war was on, to become a volunteer in Queen Mary's Army Auxiliary Service (otherwise known as the WAACs). She did not leave England for France until the early autumn of 1918, so her war service had been shorter and sweeter than Vera's, but she had shared Vera's thoughts and feelings about the war, she had volunteered, she had been in France. Vera could not forgive her and possibly never would have done so. Blows inflicted on us, however innocently, when we are in low spirits seem much heavier. She went on seeing the other woman at history coachings but not otherwise, until, some six months later, Vera was lying ill at her lodgings and she turned up bringing help and sympathy. The other woman was, of course, Winifred Holtby, bringing help when needed as she would for the next fifteen years.

It may well have been that by that stage Vera was ready to recover, but it was certainly Winifred, warm-hearted, clever, sensitive, thoughtful, from a stable home in a stable place, who completed the cure. Vera always thought that Winifred replaced for her the closeness and undemanding friendship of her brother Edward. In a sense, as long as she lived, Winifred might be said to have replaced all Vera's closest people: the dead; the Brittains, who, bereft of their son were unfailingly kind but never really understood their daughter; Vera's husband, who was away more than he was at home. Winifred, whose capacity for friendship was great and whose ability to meet the needs of others enormous, poured herself into the vacuum.

It was not a completely one-sided arrangement. When Winifred finally collapsed in tears on learning that Harry Pearson, the man she had loved since she was fifteen had become engaged to a woman he had met on a boat going to South America, it was into Vera's arms she fell. And Vera had the good sense to see that the ostensible reason for the collapse – a crisis of religious faith on Winifred's part – was not the real reason, and was accordingly kind.

When they both left Oxford with second-class degrees the two young women – Vera now aged twenty-eight, Winifred twenty-four – decided to seek their fortunes as journalists and writers. The choice was made out of enthusiasm but also, no doubt, because of all the careers available for women it was the one with most openings for women and the least sexual discrimination. It had the added advantage of not involving automatic resignation on marriage.

By 1922 they were in London, the adventure begun.

TWO

Vera and Winifred

Winifred Holtby was the first of the two daughters of Alice and David Holtby. David Holtby, a prosperous East-York-shireman, would be best described as a gentleman farmer, that is to say, he lived on his farm, took charge of it and cared for his workers but was not up every morning to milk the cows. Alice Holtby was a vigorous woman and probably the strongest influence in the family, accounting for a feminism in Winifred so unselfconscious that she scarcely accepted the label. When Winifred was twenty-five, her mother was the first woman elected to the Yorkshire County Council. In 1932 she became the first woman alderman.

Winifred grew up strong, healthy and intelligent, in the middle of a sociable family at Rudston. The house was often full, since the Holtbys entertained family and friends a great deal. Later she was to deplore the busy atmosphere and the temptations it offered when she was studying for her Oxford finals, or trying to. Later still, the demands of the family, the Yorkshire lack of distance between people and their family and friends, and the open-door policy which was part of their tradition, were to prove a burden. Nevertheless, it was probably her early life at Rudston which gave her a fundamentally trusting attitude and a pleasant, open-hearted way of dealing with others – a sense that people are connected and should help each other. At any rate Winifred's upbringing was a fortunate one in many ways. The activities of her mother, and the generally authoritative way of Yorkshirewomen, meant there was little pressure on her to conform to the passive model of women which Vera had been forced to challenge. There was, for example, no opposition when she decided to go to Oxford.

Winifred, at eleven, went to Queen Margaret's School at Scarborough, where she did well, although, horribly enough, it was at this no doubt very good school that she started on the path to her final illness. She was pale, grew fast, the climate was severe. Scarborough, on the east coast of Yorkshire, is generally considered to be a healthy, bracing spot, especially by Yorkshire people who go there on holiday and to convalesce. Anne Brontë went there for her health, although she died and is buried there. It takes a hardy constitution to withstand the east coast of Yorkshire in winter and even though Winifred came from that part of the country she was very often ill with what we should call streptococcal infections. Her neck glands were removed as the glands had swollen – not a remedy we would apply today because of its danger to the immune system. She had rheumatic fever and her final illness, years later, was attributed to this. Vera also reports in *Testament of Friendship* that there may have been something seriously wrong with the school's sanitation, since when it moved to Scotland during the First World War the girls became ill less often.

But by then the damage had been done to Winifred. She was left with an appearance of outstanding strength, good health and vitality, but with the seeds of a fatal illness lying dormant within her. She was blonde, very tall, had bright blue eyes and a clear face; Vera called her a 'Viking', yet she was to die at only thirty-seven.

But this was thirteen years away when the two young women moved into a tiny flat in Doughty Street, a location probably picked more for its literary associations than its facilities, for it was in the heart of publishing London, and Dickens had lived there. One room was partitioned, making two bedrooms. They had to crouch by the gas fire in the morning to get warm (they were used to waking to fires lit by the servants). An old woman brought up breakfast, they lunched out and made snack suppers in the evening. They did their own housework. It is not surprising that the arrangement lasted only a few months. It was followed by a move to a more spacious flat in the same house and then a further move, when they decided to opt for better conditions at the same rent in a less fashionable area. At this point Winifred's old nurse came up from Yorkshire to keep house for them. As prosperous young women they had been trained to see that a house ran properly but had no idea how to do the work themselves (when Vera began nursing in Buxton at the age of twenty-one she thought an egg could be boiled by putting it in a pan of boiling water, turning off the heat, then rescuing it three minutes later).

The servant problem always loomed large in their joint lives, yet in many other respects the world in 1922 was far more 'modern' than before the war, as if Britain had been hurled suddenly forward into the future. Perhaps it had. 'Anyone born before 1900 can examine one civilization as if it were done with,' Storm Jameson, herself born in 1891, wrote in the 1960s. The pre-war world would have struck us as Victorian; the new one had most of the features we take for granted today. It had gramophones, cinemas and cars, domestic gadgets, pop music, energetic dances, and, particularly as far as women were concerned, modern dress. Women's clothing had become less formal and restricting during the years just before the war, but if ankles had begun to show, legs certainly hadn't, hair was still long and piled up on top of the head when a girl reached womanhood, hats became obligatory at the same age and it ceased to be respectable to go without a corset of some kind. Composure was still required to keep everything in its proper place – if a woman ran, her hair became disarranged or fell down, her hat might tip sideways or fall off, her corset would make her breathless, the bottom of her dress might become wet or muddy. The crippling effect of the clothing made the wearer vulnerable: men were required to escort her from place to place, carry burdens and generally lend assistance. Obviously, all this applied more to wealthy women – the poorer ones had to manage somehow. Nevertheless, the change in women's feelings about their lives as, quite quickly, skirts crept up to above the knee, hair was bobbed and corsets became unfashionable is hard to imagine. Vera herself became a lifelong convert to cosmetics, ten years earlier a sign of moral depravity in a woman, now symbolic of freedom and modernity. Her judgement on the appearance of the unmade-up women of Hitler's Germany was unfriendly. She was just as critical about her countrywomen: 'Why, why must social reform and political intelligence in the women of this country be associated with shiny noses and unwashed hair?' she wrote.

The new, relaxed kind of dress is often put down to the need to burst out after the war and forget about death and despair. But men's clothes, although they became less formal, did not alter nearly so much as women's. Perhaps the painted faces and short skirts were just the sign of a society with too few men to go around: competition was fierce, display essential. But it may have been, too, that after the contribution they had made to the war effort and the granting of the vote to women over thirty in 1917, women felt ebullient and hopeful. Their clothes expressed this. At any rate, Vera and Winifred arrived in London just as all this was beginning. There was wild experimentation in the arts, sexual behaviour had become freer (the twenties made the permissive sixties look tepid, I was once told by someone who had experienced both decades). Perhaps most shocking to an older, conservative generation, homosexuality, a subject previously pushed firmly under the carpet, was openly discussed and written about. And for Vera and Winifred, as for many others, their sense of freedom probably emerged as the belief that, now that the war was over and women had the vote, a brave new world, socially and politically, could begin. They would help to create it.

Luckily both came from prosperous families who were willing to give them allowances while they began the adventure. Winifred's allowance was £4 a week, a sum which in those days would support a bricklayer, or a minor clerk, and his family. Vera, never very specific about her own finances, probably had about the same. The Holtbys and the Brittains must have sensibly decided to provide the bread and butter; Vera and Winifred had to earn their own jam. After a brief post-war boom, mass unemployment became a feature of the twenties (two million were unemployed by 1921). After the Wall Street Crash, during the Depression the figure rose to three million, out of a total population of forty-six million. But however good or bad their prospects might be Vera and Winifred were never going to be faced with the dole queue. If the worst came to the worst they could always go home, although that was no doubt the last thing they wanted to do.

With the move to the more comfortable flat and the installation of Winifred's old nanny as housekeeper, both women were able to hurl themselves into work. From that time on the household was never to be without servants. By the time Vera had children there was a staff of at least five: a married couple, the Burnetts, two maids and the children's nanny or, later, governess, as well as a part-time secretary for Vera and no doubt a daily woman to do the roughest work. Employing help in the house was not at the time a sign of fantastic wealth. In 1931 one in five households had at least one servant. Wages were quite low – a maid might get £1 a week, a nanny might get £2. There are times when Vera's complaints about the servant problem – they got ill, had badly timed days off and on one occasion a maid became unexpectedly pregnant – make her seem spoilt, but it has to be borne in mind that keeping house in those days was harder than it is today. It involved carrying coal, laundry work (there were no easy-care fabrics), heavy cleaning (the fires made everything more dirty), heavy cooking (there were practically no convenience foods) and a hundred and one skills acquired by the girls in poorer families from childhood onwards. Both Vera and Winifred wanted to write and be active in society. They had no domestic training. When Vera's children were born it is very doubtful whether she, or even Winifred as long as they were living together, would have been able to put sufficient effort into the rest of their lives if they had not had domestic help. 'Unless a woman is highly egotistical or highly fortunate,' wrote Winifred, 'her struggle to obtain freedom from domestic preoccupation exhausts a major part of her energy before it ever finds its way near her work.'

Meanwhile, both of them were writing novels. Winifred did tutoring, Vera taught and also began what was to prove to be a lifelong career as a public speaker. She seems to have regarded her ability to hold an audience partly as a source of pride, partly with the rueful pleasure of someone with a natural gift who would rather it had led in another direction. In particular at this time she spoke for the League of Nations, the first focus of her pacifism. In 1919 President Woodrow Wilson of the USA had put it to Congress that what was needed was an association of nations primarily designed to afford mutual guarantees of political and territorial independence to all concerned, although in the event the United States did not ratify the covenant of the League of Nations when it was set up. Based in Geneva, in neutral Switzerland, the League eventually consisted of almost forty states, predominantly European and Latin American, and included the USA. The League had inbuilt weaknesses: the membership consisted of any state which the chief members (the USA, Britain, France and Italy) wanted to include and, obviously, no state they did not want to join. Excluded, therefore, were Germany, Austria and Turkey, the former wartime enemies, and the USSR, which, after the Revolution in 1915, was establishing itself as a Communist state. The fact that only a handful of nations decided the membership, that one nation alone could veto any suggestion and, in particular, that the League had no power to enforce any suggestion or recommendation it might make, enfeebled it. Nevertheless the League of Nations initially spelt hope and perhaps at that time it was impossible to believe, after the carnage of the First World War, that the will to make it work was lacking.

The immediate post-war years were a period of hope – after all the suffering it was impossible to believe there could be any more war, that social conditions would not improve, that women, now they had the vote, would not achieve all they wanted. What happened to women immediately after the war may well have been the first indication that these hopes would not be fulfilled. There was wholesale sacking of women (such as policewomen or married women teachers) who had been doing men's jobs during the war. The London Hospital, which had trained women as doctors during the war, refused to take any more as students. 'Fear of the loss of power by those in possession of it; fear, therefore, of women,' Vera said succinctly of the situation. After that the rules about women having to retire from work when they married were fiercely applied and stayed in force until the

Second World War. Vera and Winifred both comment on the number of qualified women they knew who were either secretly married or living with a man one way or another without marriage, simply so that the woman did not have to give up her work. At first the demobilized needed jobs, so the women had to go. Later, during the Depression, it was argued that women should not be taking the jobs away from men, who were the breadwinners for whole families.

None the less, these were the days of hope. Both Vera and Winifred joined the Labour Party. Vera did so as a result of canvassing in Bethnal Green for the Liberal candidate. Conditions in the East End of London had always been bad but not many middle-class London women saw them, let alone those from Buxton. Vera, with her sharp eye for human misery developed in military hospitals,

saw the men fighting one losing battle against economic depression and increasing unemployment, while the women waged another against excessive procreation combined with an accumulation of wasteful, interminable domestic detail, and the babies fought yet a third against under-nourishment, over-clothing, perpetual dirt and inadequate fresh air and sunshine. [This, she says] did not make me philanthropically minded ... it made me politically minded once and for all; I knew that for the rest of my life I could never again feel free from the obligation of working with those who were trying to change the social system that made this grim chaos possible ...

The trio of causes both women decided to support consisted of the League of Nations, the Labour Party and the Six Point Group, begun in 1921 by Lady Rhondda, daughter of a rich coal-owner, who also helped to found *Time and*

Tide, the radical all-women magazine to which so many of the gifted women of the time contributed. Considering some of the six points the Group thought worth fighting for provides some clues to the world in which women were then living.

A battle they won with difficulty was to raise the age of consent from thirteen to sixteen. They struggled to make both parents equally the guardians of their children, to secure equal pay for men and women teachers and equality of opportunity in the Civil Service. The aim of stopping the sacking of married women in public service was achieved but women still had to leave when they had children. The difficulties of achieving a proper education or training, and the impossibility of staying in a white-collar job after marriage or, in teaching and the Civil Service, after having a child, on the whole drove women into low-paid jobs and away from any notion of a career. Vera and Winifred, keen proponents of equality, were personally better off in the more egalitarian world of freelance writers.

In 1923 both published their first novels. After many rejections, Vera's *The Dark Tide* found a publisher, Grant Richards, although she had to subsidize the cost of publication herself. The book came out in July and met with a fairly tepid critical response ('Some day she might write a good book,' faint-praised the *Saturday Review*). The attitudes of the critics are fairly understandable. *The Dark Tide* begins in Oxford, where Daphne Lethbridge, described as being physically rather like Winifred Holtby, albeit a much more uncertain, less optimistic woman than the model, meets Virginia Dennison, who is physically like Vera Brittain herself: small, dark, rather chic. Virginia is her own woman, in contrast to the unconfident Daphne. When she decides, in spite of having got a first-class degree, to train as a nurse and eventually takes off for the typhoid epidemic in post-revolutionary Russia, the reader can easily believe in this strong, self-determining character (she is very much the 'other woman' of a woman's youth – the friend without doubts about her appearance, views or decisions).

Daphne falls in love with her tutor, who teaches both her and Virginia, but it is to Virginia that he proposes marriage. Virginia refuses him. Out of pique he proposes to Daphne, who accepts him, although she senses he does not love her. In a misguided attempt to gain his respect by academic success she drives herself to try and get a first – and makes herself so nervous she does badly in the examination. Failure succeeds failure. The marriage is not a success. When the married couple begin their life in London Vera was evidently out of her depth in terms of her own experience, and so she falls back on melodrama and conventional plot ingredients. Daphne conceives but her husband declares he is in love with an opera singer and leaves. Alone, she goes into labour and is unable to summon help. Virginia arrives at the last moment but the child, a son, is born crippled. Meanwhile Daphne sues for divorce but, since her husband is standing for Parliament, the scandal of a divorce involving his adultery will ruin his chances. His mistress arrives and pleads with Daphne, who agrees not to go ahead with the case. The book concludes with some of that Edwardian overwriting of which Vera Brittain was always guilty when she felt uncertain of her own ground and wanted to batter herself, and the reader, into belief:

How could there be anything splendid in what she had done, she who had acquiesced meekly in a sordid compromise, who had allowed love's jewels to be trampled in the dust? . . . From the half-open door of her bedroom came a faint, plaintive sound; her crippled son was moaning a little in his sleep.

The earlier parts of the book – the lacerating picture of the young woman who is getting everything wrong, the conversations between the friends – do have some merit. Later the book descends into purple passages and Edwardian plot cliché. In *The Dark Tide* Vera was trying to write like an *ingénue*, writing away from her central preoccupation, which was the terrible past, ignoring the years when every assumption created by a prosperous middle-class upbringing was overturned.

It would be easy to argue that she was not a natural novelist. Except in the case of *Honourable Estate*, written under the stress of personal emotion and dealing with the two subjects with which she was most emotionally involved – the position of women and the never-forgotten experiences of war – in her fiction she seems, almost wilfully to write away from the subjects she felt most deeply about and, when she does approach them, veers off again in apparent terror. Perhaps this creates a lack of tension in the subject matter, and, feeling she should be putting more into it, she tries to make up for this by overwriting in the old-fashioned style. Sometimes the tone of her novels makes the reader wonder if she had not taken one too many lessons from the hyperbolic Marie Connor Leighton. It was her mediocre reception as a novelist she thought of when brooding on her unasked-for talent as a public speaker, but in a sense she was perhaps never destined to be a novelist at all: her real interests did not lie in that direction. Her gift was for politics and society, for seeing problems and finding solutions. She did not even seem to read very much fiction. The charge once made against Winifred, that she was a confirmed middle-brow, is just as true of her friend Vera.

Nevertheless, Winifred's *Anderby Wold*, which she started writing at Oxford, easily found a publisher (John Lane), came out in March and got a better reception than *The Dark Tide* – something of a test of friendship when both authors are in their twenties and living together in one flat. *Anderby Wold* is an impressive achievement from a woman of twenty-four.

The novel may be partly valedictory, for by the end of the First World War Winifred's father, unable to cope with modern labour demands, had sold his land and the house at Rudston where Winifred had grown up; she had lost her rural childhood and the solidity of traditional Yorkshire land-owning life and had been moved to a semi-suburban background. (In fact both Winifred's and Vera's fathers, though fairly young men, had sold up the family home and given up active work. David Holtby's decision may have been partly based on the fact that he had no son to take over the farm; Thomas Brittain's on the fact that his only son, Edward, showed no signs of wanting to be an active director in the paper mill.) Mary Robson, in *Anderby Wold*, is dedicated to her own farm. She has unsentimentally married her cousin, who will work the land with her. They have managed to pay off a mortgage but there are two things against her

now: after ten years of marriage she has no child, and therefore no son to inherit the land, and the old feudal ways are
being questioned. Then, by accident, she meets a young
radical, the man who calls her 'a benevolent despot'. Up to
now her passion has been centred on her land, but she falls
in love with him.

Anderby Wold is a very grown-up novel for a young
woman in her early twenties to have considered writing. It
lacks the obligatory autobiographical heroine of youthful
fiction – Mary Robson, proud, obstinate, in love with her
farm, is not Winifred Holtby. It lacks sentimentality – the
land is hard, the villagers fair but sceptical and deeply
conservative, the Robson relatives are inhibited, cannot
show love, do not wish their own blood any harm, but quite
enjoy seeing someone get their come-uppance, especially
when they predicted it beforehand. 'It'll be worse if you
don't yield,' says Mary Robson's sister-in-law, warning her
to sell the farm, giving her the hard truth, Yorkshire-style.
And she is right, of course – the man she loves, Rossitur,
dies a violent death and the farm is lost. Yet if the theme is
sad and the approach unromantic much of the time, the
novel still belongs to the light and not the dark. It is full of
life and observation, although, ambiguously, behind the
appreciation of life in Winifred's novels there always lies the
feeling that happiness is elusive and ordinary satisfactions
are not to be had.

The figure of Rossitur, the stranger and intellectual, re-
appears in Winifred's third novel, *The Land of Green Ginger*,
as Paul Szermei. He is not an autobiographical hero; Harry
Pearson, with whom Winifred was in love, was the son of a

local bank manager, a childhood friend. The mysterious figure who arrives in the cut-off Yorkshire settings of *Anderby Wold* and *The Land of Green Ginger* with information from the outside is more likely to be a dream figure from girlhood, the sexual and intellectual liberator, almost magically coming along to release the young woman from the bonds, however pleasant and reassuring they might be, of life in commonsensical Yorkshire. He is, like Ladislaw in George Eliot's *Middlemarch*, a thinking man, a romantic stranger and, by virtue of his foreignness, totally uncommitted to the conventions of British society.

Both Vera and Winifred came from the solid school of provincial novelists – as did their friends and acquaintances, J. B. Priestley and Phyllis Bentley – working in the same style, with an emphasis on straightforward narrative carrying plot, character and moral within it. They were light years away from the impressionistic or experimental, the cynical, the daring or the bold work of their contemporaries. Proust and Joyce were both contemporaries, as were Scott Fitzgerald, Aldous Huxley, Virginia Woolf, D. H. Lawrence. There are shadings in Winifred Holtby's work indicating that for her the world of *Middlemarch* was no longer everything, but on the whole, as writers, both women stuck to the mainstream of British fiction: the social novel. Nevertheless, at this stage Winifred's was the more developed talent, although her books were increasingly to show signs of the almost legendary distractions the author permitted herself or could not prevent. Both women, in fact, took it quite for granted, as many authors do not, that while writing a book they would also accept public speaking engagements, take a holiday, go off lecturing, attend a few parties, write a few articles, go to a conference. Their motives were sometimes financial, since both were maintaining themselves by journalism, but another reason may well have been that as well as being writers they were also women, reared to expect their time to be broken up by inescapable family duties – as, indeed, it was – so that they took it for granted that human beings, whether making claims on their time in the form of politics, family or friendship, were just as inevitable and important as literary work.

In January 1924 Vera published her second book, *Not Without Honour* (the word 'honour' appears several times in her book titles). The heroine Christine Merivale is plainly autobiographical; the action takes place in the dark days before Oxford when Vera was the 'home daughter' waiting for a husband. Describing her heroine, on public display, she writes:

Christine, mutinously silent, felt more like a dressed-up doll than ever. A doll being turned over and priced by other people . . . A doll put up to auction in the market place, waiting to be flung at the head of the highest bidder . . . Nobody at Torborough seemed to have realised that these were the days of Woman's just claim to equality with Man.

Christine (as Vera once did, plainly the memory was still strong) falls in love with the married vicar, whose wife is rather vulgar and unsympathetic. The vicar (as Vera's vicar apparently was) is dismissed from the parish for disconcerting his comfortable congregation with his radical sermons. In *Not Without Honour* he delivers a final sermon, not intended to be ironic, comparing himself with the crucified Christ. Christine impulsively offers herself to him but he backs off. Her parents hear of this and forbid her ever to see him again. She escapes them and runs to her intended lover, suggesting he should divorce his wife for her, but again he evades her. She goes to Oxford and, while there, hears he has died in the trenches. He has left a meaningful letter behind for her – it is as if his letter and his sacrificial death redeem him after his rejection of her. The whole book has more attack and coherence than *The Dark Tide*, although it is often hard to see how far, as readers, we are intended to sympathize with the main characters, how far intended to see them neutrally. Yet, again, the feeling is that the writer is not fully in creative touch with the material. It was to be ten years before Vera Brittain wrote another novel.

If *Not Without Honour* went unhailed, the author had other things to occupy her mind. She was just thirty and her life was about to change radically. The previous June she had been sent a card by a young lecturer in politics and economics who had spotted her while she was in Oxford with Winifred, said he thought he had seen her before at Somerville debates and wondered if she would like to come to tea or go on the river with him. This invitation to a typical Oxford courtship she could not accept, as she was then in London. A few months later he wrote to her about her novel and sent her a monograph he had written. She replied, but his response, prefiguring the future, came from a boat heading for America. The young man was, of course, her husband-to-be, George Catlin (whom she always called Gordon). Correspondence raged between them for a whole year, during which time George extended his contract as a lecturer at Cornell University. In spite of the fact that he had done this and that they had, seemingly, never met, Vera nevertheless wrote to Winifred, then in Yorkshire, in December 1923, the day before her birthday,

I have had another long letter from Mr Catlin – intimate and amazingly interesting. Isn't it queer that I don't even know what he looks like. You know I feel vaguely uneasy and rather miserable. I do hope that, after this lovely period of peace, some devastating male is not going to push into my life and upset it again.

'I cannot help thinking that you can yourself prevent them from being devastating,' Winifred sensibly wrote back. But by the time George Catlin returned to Britain in June 1924 it was plain that devastation was on the way.

Vera contrived to miss him at the first meeting, although she must have known that after a year's correspondence this maidenly behaviour was not likely to put him off. That propriety satisfied, the couple spent the weekend together in London. Vera knew that George was planning to propose marriage to her. Because it was the anniversary of Edward's death she felt the moment was particularly appropriate. This idea was probably one of a complicated set of thoughts concerning what it meant to start a new life with a man when so many men from the old life, Roland in particular, had died. The war, and the dead, were perhaps never going to be far from Vera's sexual and emotional life. It looks very much as if the surfacing of sexual feeling, which was obviously not openly acknowledged in girls or by them at that time and was therefore more shattering when it came, followed by the almost instantaneous death of her lover, set up a chain of associations in her mind so that for ever she would associate sexual love with death, with the battlefields of northern France and with war. No one had been able to comfort her sufficiently when the tragedies occurred; no one had talked to her about it at the time; the term 'survivor guilt' would not be generally used for fifty years. She seems certainly to have thought that from Roland's death onward she was emotionally burnt out. Somehow, when she says George was about to propose on the anniversary of Edward's death, it is as if she were telling herself that even if a new life was beginning, she had not forgotten the old one.

The next weekend at Oxford George did propose and Vera accepted. They had spent, by then, about five days together, but they had been corresponding for a year – the courtship had taken place by post; the meetings were just confirmation of an agreement they must have been reaching over many months. George, fair, handsome, gifted intellectually and at the start of what looked like a promising career (he was two and a half years younger than Vera) was what, in Buxton, would have been seen as a 'catch'. The marriage, in spite of partings, arguments and the like, lasted a lifetime.

A year's engagement followed, for George had to leave for Cornell University in September. Vera and Winifred went to the League of Nations convention in Switzerland, which they tried never to miss, and then to Czechoslovakia, Austria and Hungary. When they returned to London, life went on as usual until June. Then George arrived and the marriage took place at St James's, Spanish Place, in the West End of London – George Catlin was a Roman Catholic.

The Leightons came to the wedding. Vera gave her bouquet to Marie Leighton afterwards. (For Vera exchanges of flowers as gifts, as thanks, at weddings and funerals always had great significance.) 'Her cheeks were thickly smudged with brick-coloured rouge which contrasted oddly with the long locks of saffron-yellow hair hanging unevenly beneath the incredible hat,' she wrote cruelly thirty years later. But however undignified Marie Leighton's appearance during this sombre renunciation, the scene meant for Vera that the past was over, reconciled, though still remembered, and a new life was beginning.

THREE

Vera, George and Winifred

If she was less romantically in love with George Catlin than she had been with Roland Leighton, one thing had not changed. Years before, when younger and more passionately in love, she had tried to assure herself that Roland Leighton would not try to prevent her from pursuing a career. Now she was anxious that George would accept a working wife. 'I want to solve the problem of how a married woman, without being inordinately rich, can have children and yet retain her intellectual and spiritual independence as well as having time for the pursuit of her own career,' she wrote to George Catlin, before the marriage. The problems of home, family and career have hardly been solved for women today, but at that time the domestic load was more weighty and so, seemingly, were the more metaphysical burdens. Marriage involved a complete, almost religious, commitment on the woman's side. The domestic responsibilities, heavy in themselves, also symbolized complete dedication. Thus Storm Jameson, although a woman of huge physical energy, when faced with setting up a home for herself and her husband was always seized with mad confusion very like that of a cat being thrust into a basket. 'Domestic preoccupation exhausts a major part of [a woman's] energy,' said Winifred; it was not what the women were asked to do, but what they were asked to feel about it which put them in such a state of panic.

Thus Vera, for whom life without marriage and children would have been a terrible deprivation, asked George, as she had earlier asked Roland, for his tolerance of her work. She may have been ahead of her time, but not so far ahead that it occurred to her to ask either man for active help. Even among these liberal thinkers, there was never any hope of practical domestic equality.

The marriage, begun by Vera in the belief that she would never feel deep romantic love again (it would have been like betraying her dead) seems to have got off to a rocky start. The couple honeymooned in Austria, Hungary and Yugoslavia. George, as he always would, took the chance to go and interview politicians and influential men. Vera had the English romantic habit of describing her emotional state in terms of the weather and the landscape, so it is disconcerting to find her account of the honeymoon dominated by menacing cliffs, gloomy sunsets, overhanging gorges, smouldering clouds and blinding rain. The record begins, 'After a rainy weekend in Dover we travelled to Vienna,' and ends in the Alps with 'the restless Romanche tumbling in petulant cascades over its rocky bed.' The couple then had to rush home, as Vera's aunt had committed suicide. By the time Vera had reached the seventh anniversary of the marriage she was able to write, 'So glad it is now and not then, when we were both so unadjusted – both mentally and physically.'

Winifred, meanwhile, was very unhappy. She and Vera had been each other's chief intellectual resource, companion and support-system for three years. From now on Vera would be living in the U S A. She would probably have children. The relationship was effectively over. Friends rallied round, Vera's parents invited Winifred to stay at their flat so that she would not be alone, but her real salvation was to be the six months she spent in South Africa from January 1926 onwards.

It has been said – and was said by gossips at the time – that Vera and Winifred had a lesbian relationship. Proof that two people have *not* been lovers is always hard to come by, but it certainly seems highly unlikely that Vera and Winifred had any such relationship. The whole tone and quality of the friendship argue against it. Winifred died with Harry Pearson's name on her lips. Vera married and had children. Moreover, Vera's attitude to homosexuality in men or women appears to have been compassionate and liberal at a time when compassion and liberality were probably less available than they are today (male homosexuality was punishable by law), but it does not seem to have been partisan. In 1928 she was asked by the defence to give evidence for the writer Radclyffe Hall, whose lesbian novel *The Well of Loneliness* had been stopped on grounds of obscenity. She was probably asked to speak for the book because of her earlier review of it in *Time and Tide.* Here she had begun briskly by saying that if the style and organization of the novel were open to criticism, it

can only strengthen the belief of all honest and courageous persons that there is no problem which is not better frankly stated than concealed. Persecution and disgusted ostracism have never solved any problem in the world and they do not make the position of the female invert less bitter to herself or less dangerous to others ... Women of the type of Stephen Gordon (lesbian heroine of the novel) deserve the fullest consideration and compassion from all who are fortunate enough to have escaped one of Nature's cruellest dispensations.

The response to the very painful, semi-autobiographical novel may be somewhat pompous, but it is compassionate; it is that of a natural libertarian and hater of persecution and social hypocrisy. It is also markedly heterosexual. In the event, the case collapsed before any of the writers came to give evidence. *The Well of Loneliness* was banned and the judge, at appeal, described it as 'more subtle, demoralising, corrosive and corrupting than anything that was ever written'.

Winifred's novel *The Crowded Street* had come out the previous year, she was making a name for herself as a journalist, but her best friend had gone, seemingly for ever. *The Crowded Street* is not her best book; she herself declared it to be a partial failure. Its interest perhaps lies in the fact that it is another 'home daughter' novel, like *Not Without Honour*, and as Winifred said, the character of Muriel is a portrait of 'the stupid, frightened part of myself': the part she and Vera had gone to Oxford, and then together to London, to escape.

In 1925 she was desolate. Six months in South Africa, travelling and lecturing at least took her away and gave her fresh interests. After a few months she began to see the power of white men, the boredom and frustration of white women and, of course, the racial injustice. She may not have got the situation quite right, for she believed the country to be on the verge of revolution. If it seems odd that the situation in South Africa was something of a revelation to Winifred, we have to remember again that there was no instant information through television, that a third of the globe was 'painted red', as used to be said (the colour used to show the British Empire) and that most of the inhabitants of Great Britain took it completely for granted that their Government should be in charge of millions of men and women of other races. Although not ill-informed, it may well be that Winifred's mental picture of the condition of subject races had been based on the poor of rural Yorkshire, where poverty and oppression were not so bad and there was some hope of relief by squirearchical intervention or social legislation. For the rest of her life Winifred was committed to working for better conditions in South Africa. The prospects may even have looked more hopeful at that time, before apartheid and pass laws were introduced.

On her return to Britain in May 1926 she was almost immediately appointed a director of *Time and Tide*, the magazine about which, only a few years before, Vera Brittain had pleaded, 'Leave *Time and Tide* alone for a bit; you mayn't be quite their style.' In spite of her influential job, Winifred, being only twenty-eight, could not vote, since the age for women's voting still stood at thirty. Two years later women got equal voting rights, with men.

She now knew Vera was coming back to England. Although Vera's had seemed the success story of the friendship – she was the one who married and went away – she had not been very happy during her year in the States. She found Cornell University restrictive, the society of male academics excluded women, and the couple were living on $750 a year, which was not enough for Vera to go on trips when George travelled, nor to employ much domestic help, which was anyway less available in America than in England. She did embark on a book entitled *Honeymoon in Two Continents*. She certainly planned the idea for a novel set between 1913 and 1919, which she had mentioned in a letter to Winifred some two years previously. This was the book she was not destined to write for ten years. In the meanwhile, her books and the articles she wrote were turned down. A move to New York, where George obtained a post researching Prohibition, made little difference. The scene she describes in *Testament of Experience* where she sat typing out her husband's book, *The Science and Method of Politics*, during a hot New York summer seems to sum up her feelings of personal frustration. Her duty, as it would then have been seen, was to stay with her husband and support him in his career. In fact she returned permanently to Britain in August.

Writing in 1938 of her first experience of America and her return to Britain, she says bluntly of this decision,

Looking back on that part of my life which I have already fulfilled, I realise that its most valuable turning points have always followed some refusal to accommodate myself to circumstances which I found hampering, uncongenial or oppressive. I have had constantly to choose between being disagreeable and becoming ineffective.

By this time, twelve years after a choice she must have

made with some uncertainty, the decision had in some ways justified itself. In her forties she was a successful author, mother of well-grown children, still married to the man she was separating from in 1926. She had done it her way. So, in the same section of the book she can write vigorously, and much of it can be taken as the philosophy by which she lived,

In one of the religious books which pious relatives were accustomed to present to girls of my generation at the time of their confirmation I remember reading an injunction to the effect that we ought to cultivate 'those virtues which grow at the foot of the Cross' – patience, meekness, self-effacement, the capacity for acceptance. I should like to ram that falsehood down the throat of the unctuous moralist who penned it. Nothing could be more destructive of character and more warping to vitality than a long course of abnegation and sacrifice. Were it not for this universal inertia of humble, patient acceptance, the worst human evils – war, cruelty, poverty, the oppression of the penniless and the persecution of the weak – could be destroyed tomorrow. In the world as I have come to know it I have come to recognise resignation as the deadliest of the seven deadly sins.

Nevertheless, what was presented later as a decision made rationally and easily, on the basis of facts, was not really like that. As early as October, not long after arriving in the States, she wrote to Winifred suggesting that she would return to London for the next autumn and winter. Gradually, as the year wore on her attitude became firmer. By June she was telling Winifred she planned to base herself in England for the next five years. By July some uncertainty appears in her letters about whether she and Winifred could, so to speak, pick up where they left off, go on in the same flat in the same way. Perhaps for her part Winifred was unsure about whether the plan would work, whether, by this stage, she even wanted it to, and where George would fit into the arrangements. Nevertheless, when Vera returned she and Winifred went back to living in the same flat on the same footing, while a postal row went on between Vera and George. From America he protested about what seemed, matrimonially speaking, to be a very unsatisfactory state of affairs. Permanent separation seemed to be on the cards, but the danger was somehow averted – the 'part-time marriage' as Vera called it, was under weigh. From that point on, and for many years to come, Vera and George would be apart during the academic terms at Cornell University and often during the vacations, since the boat between Britain and the USA took a week, making meetings expensive and difficult.

It is easy to see that a marriage based on so little personal contact before the wedding, followed by a whirlwind honeymoon in several European countries and a move to another continent, could run into trouble. Vera's capacity for rapid thought, planning and action may for once have done her no good, if, as it seems, this capacity conflicted with the ordinary facts of life or, perhaps, with her husband's nature. Not everyone can adapt so quickly to change. But in the end it was her ability to follow up rapid resolutions with practical answers, organization and dogged hard work which probably saved the marriage. She stuck out the year in the USA, came back to Britain, saved the marriage on what looks like, at that time, her own terms, restored her close companionship with Winifred, who is beginning now to look like her *alter ego*, and was to continue her career, bear and rear her children and continue the marriage successfully. A lesser woman would have failed to succeed in at least one of these objectives.

During the following spring she returned to America and not long afterwards found that she was pregnant. She came back to Britain in the summer, the part-time marriage now a *fait accompli*, as she and Winifred together moved to a bigger flat to make room for the coming baby.

That autumn Winifred published *The Land of Green Ginger*, which is, I think, perhaps her best novel. Her last book, *South Riding*, is better known, wider in scope and more widely read, but *The Land of Green Ginger* is more 'felt'. It cuts deeper. The book is set in Yorkshire, like *Anderby Wold*, but the position of the heroine is grimmer. Far from being a strongly rooted, landowning woman, Joanna Burton was born in South Africa, the daughter of a missionary. She is running a small farm in Yorkshire with her ex-serviceman husband, Teddy, who is consumptive (and in those days, therefore, likely to die). Because he is so ill, because of the poverty of the farm and because she has also to care for her daughters, Joanna's life is very hard. She is only too glad to take in a lodger, the Hungarian supervisor of a group of Finns hired to do forestry work in the area. Paul Szermei, the fascinating, disruptive, liberating foreigner, falls in love with her. The villagers, unsentimentally described as malicious and xenophobic – the xenophobia extending to Joanna and her husband, not just Szermei – claim she and Szermei are lovers; her sick husband becomes depressed. She cannot sleep with him: the doctor has forbidden it; his feverish jealousy, partly due to his fear he is dying, repels her; and she is terrified that he will infect her and double the chances of their children catching TB. However, she finally yields to him (Winifred, always somewhat self-conscious about her own lack of sexual experience, seems to have understood sexual and emotional matters very well). When she conceives and her husband dies the local people are certain she is bearing Szermei's child. Poor, disliked and now with three children, she sells the farm. She and her children set sail for South Africa, to seek a new life.

The novel may be flawed – the writer was an almost unbelievably busy woman of only twenty-nine – but it is fundamentally serious, totally unsentimental and truthful. The book may also be the best portrait we have of Winifred herself, for it seems fairly obvious that Joanna – kindly, overwhelmed, disorganized, looking for something better, struggling with her own resentment, seeking the light, passionately and despairingly fond of her children, aston-ished when she, knowing herself untidy, exhausted and distracted, becomes the object of the passionate love of her husband and Szermei – is not just the picture of a character in a novel. It seems to be Winifred's self-portrait – not the Winifred of Vera's naturally overdone memorial of her in *Testament of Friendship*; not the woman so often described by those who knew her as 'an angel'. Joanna may be Winifred as she, quite realistically, saw herself, with her own faults and virtues: her acceptance of hardship; her moral resolve; an almost mystical belief in the importance of being good, doing right, not failing in your duty to others; her passion and, above all, her capacity to feel joy, sometimes in very terrible circumstances. If Harry Pearson had married her, if they had spent his ex-serviceman's gratuity on a small farm in Yorkshire, if children had been born – Winifred might have been Joanna Burton. This may well be the Winifred Vera knew best but could not describe fully in *Testament of Friendship*, which was written under the eagle eye of Alice Holtby, Winifred's mother, who actually died just as Vera finished the book.

Vera and George's first child, a son, John, was born towards the end of December 1927, a week before Vera's own thirty-fourth birthday. The event took on the nature of a crisis. The baby was premature and born quickly. The nursing staff left her alone too long, the doctor arrived too late. Vera took it to heart on behalf of all women, especially the overburdened poor, with bad housing, less information about and access to contraception and very little chance of getting anaesthetics in childbirth, particularly as most of their children would be born at home. Vera, in a nursing home, obviously expected pain relief during her labour but, because of the confusion, evidently got none, or not nearly as much as she expected. Since the drug administered was most usually chloroform or powerfully narcotic chloral, modern medicine might be dubious about the general benefits, but Vera remained a strong advocate of anaesthesia in childbirth, as anyone might in a society where women did not have the luxury of choice and anaesthetics were more withheld from women than thrust upon them. 'I wanted to battle down the solid walls of the Ministry of Health,' she wrote, 'to take the Minister himself and give him a woman's inside and compel him to have six babies, all without anaesthetics.'

Matters did not improve. George had to return to the States when John was a month old, leaving Vera to cope with a frail, premature child, during an exceptionally cold winter, helped by the inexperienced Winifred and a character described as an 'untrained nursemaid'. Motherhood is a complicated skill, learned by women from each other; if there is no teacher, a woman feels very uncertain, especially as she is practising on the body of her own first child. In the year John was born sixty-nine children in every 1,000 died before they were a year old (in 1983 four children in every 1,000 died) and premature babies were particularly at risk. During the first few months of John's life Vera, and Winifred to some extent, must have put much of their youthful freedom behind them. Winifred fell in love with the baby, and was a good friend to him for as long as she lived, able to appreciate and cherish what was essentially a sensitive personality. However, she had to rush back to Yorkshire before he was three months old because her sister Grace was dying after giving birth to her own child. Vera, alone, even for a relatively short time, had a baptism of fire into being what we, ungrammatically, term these days a one-parent family. It was not for many years that George was able to give up his job in America, so the core of the household was usually Vera and Winifred, with Vera's children. It was less unusual than it might seem today. The habit we associate with Victorian families of bunching up into large family groups for social and domestic convenience still obtained and the war had left many single women – the widows, the women who would now never marry, the lonely sisters – living together.

Vera's book *Halcyon, or The Future of Monogamy*, which she wrote after John's birth, is quite an interesting bit of science fiction. Purporting to be written by a certain Professor Minerva Huxterwin (an amalgamation of the names of the scientists Huxley and Darwin), it discusses, as if in retrospect, marriage in the twentieth and twenty-first centuries. Most of Vera's faith in the future of marriage is pinned on reform in the areas of better sexual instruction, birth control and easier divorce. More eccentrically, she points out that with developments like radio, television and the cinema, and much faster transport from place to place, the couple will more easily be able to get away from each other, mentally or physically. Otherwise, the future she describes is quite conventional: after a period of promiscuity caused by the new freedom, monogamy re-establishes itself as the best way.

No type of union [she writes rather stiffly, as Minerva Huxterwin] had yet been discovered in which the maximum of intellectual variety may be so effectively combined with the minimum of emotional disturbance. No other relationship appears so well fitted to leave the mind free from the fret of sexual urge by adequately satisfying the demands of the body without giving to them that degree of attention which renders sex an incubus rather than an inspiration to mankind.

Faith in how far this brave new world advances to meet the world as we know it fails further when the recommendations also turn out to include the arranging of 'second contracts' for married men living apart from their wives – a safe, hygienic and legal solution to the problem of men without women, but which does not really take into account

81

either of the women concerned. *Halcyon* is in fact rather a stuffy book, although the predictions about the dates of various reforms, like the abolition of restrictions on married women's employment and the arrival of divorce by consent are very accurate. Perhaps the stuffiness is partly because it fails to suggest solutions for the actual difficulties besetting Vera herself at the time – how to pay the bills, keep on working and care for the house and children.

In November 1929 she began to work on her most famous book, *Testament of Youth*, and, also, three weeks later, discovered that she was pregnant again. For the next three years she was to work on *Testament of Youth*, which was finally 600 pages long and contained 250,000 words – about four times the length of an average book. The story begins with her childhood, focuses strongly on her experiences in the First World War and ends with her marriage to George Catlin.

The idea was not completely original. The years immediately preceding Vera's start on *Testament of Youth* had seen the publication of long-deferred works of autobiography and fiction concerned with the war: Robert Graves's autobiography *Goodbye To All That*, Ernest Hemingway's novel *A Farewell to Arms*, Erich Maria Remarque's novel *All Quiet on the Western Front* and R. C. Sheriff's play *Journey's End*. The works were sad, they showed the futility of war and the stupidity of the leadership and they all recalled the unforgotten dead. They had not been written earlier because the participants had had to come to terms with the horror, because at last the public was ready to hear how bad and stupid the affair had been, because only now did people see that the so-called 'sacrifice' had not changed or improved the world. The same was true for Vera Brittain. At intervals from 1923 in letters to Winifred she had been shaping and reshaping the material she so desperately needed to deal with. She knew she had never quite been able to find the right framework, which is often a sign an author is not ready to write whatever it is he or she has in mind. In practical terms this was not the best moment to begin such a long work, demanding so much detail and concentration. She slogged on for the next three years against a background of pregnancy, childbirth and the inevitable demands of bringing up young children – childish ailments, shopping trips and the occasional collapse of child-care arrangements, which happens even to the employers of many servants. At the same time she had to keep writing for newspapers and magazines to pay the bills, although, late in the day, a timely gift of £500 from her father (worth about fifty times as much now) must have eased much of the strain. Nevertheless, she wrote probably her two best books during her children's early years.

As all the other books about the war had been written by men, one of the reasons, ostensibly, why Vera wrote *Testament of Youth* was to stress the part played by women in the war. However, if this were part of her motive, it was probably only a small part (in fact she barely refers to women's role during those years). The rest was a, mostly implicit, indictment of the war itself which was intended to bear witness to the past, to celebrate the dead and, perhaps, to exorcize her own pain. In addition, she had been terrified by the disappearance of so many male figures in her life –

her reaction to her father's death and her husband's illness later proves this. At the time she began to write, she was the mother of a two-year-old son: the fact that she was now the mother of a potential soldier may very well have influenced her. Curiously enough, though, if the idea of the book was to produce a plea against war, to show what women, and Vera in particular, had done and could do, the most potent and abiding image in the book is still the image of the young woman in her nurse's uniform, tending wounded men to assuage grief because her lover has been killed. It is the classic image of women mourning husbands, sons and lovers killed in war, and tending the survivors: an image that is not intrinsically anti-war or pro-women's emancipation. Whether it was the image uppermost in Vera's mind as she wrote, or merely the one we have seized on, is another question. The book is also about survival, even resurrection, as its form shows. Like a symphony it begins with peace and calm, is succeeded by crisis and disaster and ends with re-conciliation. 'A record of spiritual growth . . . a memorial to sacrifices nobly made . . . a testimony to the horror and waste of war,' wrote *The Times Literary Supplement* reviewer of the book in 1933. But if Vera had wished to write only of the horrors of war she would have ended the book in 1918; instead a full third of the book deals with the post-war period, when she returned to Oxford, went to London and worked there, met and married her husband.

As she was writing the opening of *Testament of Youth* another move had to be made to provide more space for the new baby. This time she and Winifred moved to a house in Glebe Place in Chelsea. Conventionally it is the woman writer who struggles to complete her book before the birth of the child; in this case the struggler was Winifred, who managed to finish her novel *Poor Caroline* just ahead of the birth, in July, of Vera's daughter Shirley, named, says Vera sternly, after the bold heroine of Charlotte Brontë's novel, in case anyone should think it was Shirley Temple.

The years at Glebe Place were eventful ones. Not all the events were good. The first bad news came with Winifred's attack of illness in 1930 after flying to Lady Rhondda's house in the South of France, where *Time and Tide* staff often holidayed. After her recovery nothing was thought of this sickness until, the following year, it happened again. She had been at Glebe Place taking care of the children while George and Vera were in France. They came back suddenly because, after the resignation of Ramsay MacDonald, Labour leader of a coalition government, George had the chance to be selected as a prospective Parliamentary candidate for the Labour Party to fight the coming general election. He fought a West London constituency. Both Vera and Winifred flung themselves into the campaign. Winifred spoke for Labour in various parts of the country and even took over meetings for George and Vera when needed. A few days after the election, which George lost, the victim of a general Conservative walk-over, Winifred became very ill and collapsed. The doctor's verdict was overwork and she went to stay in the Chilterns, at Monks Risborough, overlooking the Vale of Aylesbury. Her hosts were Clare Leighton, Roland's sister and by then a fairly celebrated woodcut artist, and Noel Brailsford, the distinguished socialist writer and editor.

Winifred was still ill when she returned to London, and again collapsed. Vera took her off to another nursing home, at Sidmouth, where she had a convalescent holiday with Vera. After this she went back to a cottage in Monks Risborough, close to Clare Leighton and Noel Brailsford, where she spent four months trying to recover from the illness, now diagnosed as high blood pressure. This was indeed one of the symptoms, but treating the symptom did no good. Those months in the country, during a cold, dark part of the year, must have been lonely and frightening. Vera, who had caught chicken-pox from John, was first ill and then in quarantine and so could not visit her. At the end of the winter an event took place which Winifred only revealed three years later. By that time she had spoken to a specialist who told her she had only two more years to live. Walking alone one morning, as she broke the ice on a trough for the young lambs to drink from, she heard a voice inside her saying, 'Having nothing, and yet possessing all things' – the words of St Paul in his second letter to the Corinthians, where, in a long, inspiring passage he tells his followers of the sufferings they may have to endure for their faith and to expect no reward but the knowledge that they are doing what they must. From this point on, after what seems to have been a revelation, she was partly reconciled. She had a bad time, alone and ill at the cottage, but presumably would have been worse off in London, where she slept near the top of the house, and therefore the children, and would have been disturbed by their early rising. The servants would have had to climb flights of stairs with food and coals for the fire. London itself was, at that time, no place for an invalid in winter – the air was smoke-laden and unhealthy fogs which crept through the houses were frequent. In those days when antibiotics were unknown the best remedies for weakened patients were still the old ones of pure country air, warmth, rest and careful nursing.

However, perhaps if Winifred had been in London and if Vera had not become ill herself, she might have seen a specialist earlier. In the event Clare Leighton appears to have found one after Winifred had been ill all winter in Monks Risborough without showing any improvement. It must have been after this doctor had given Winifred only a few years to live that Vera records, having met Clare and Winifred at his office for the consultation, 'Halls Dally thought W[inifred]'s condition fairly serious but she didn't seem to mind much, thinking him a fool.' Winifred then went back to the cottage, Vera says in *Testament of Friendship*, although from her diary it seems she in fact went into a clinic for more tests.

Vera's response to all this was peculiar. Immediately after the consultation with the doctor she invited Winifred's friend, the novelist Phyllis Bentley, a Yorkshirewoman whom Vera did not know at all, to come and stay at Glebe Place. Phyllis Bentley's latest book *Inheritance*, which now, with its three generations of Yorkshire folk and 'trouble at t'mill', seems to the modern reader something of a cliché, had become a best seller. The critics mostly raved about it, Winifred loved it, Vera wept as she read; only the tough-minded Rebecca West disliked it, calling it conventional and sedative, perhaps the verdict we would agree with today. Nevertheless, the book went into edition after edition. Vera was fascinated by its success. Phyllis Bentley, though slightly startled by this invitation from a stranger, accepted. Vera met her from the same train Winifred usually took and they went back to the house, where Phyllis was installed in Winifred's room. There were parties, since Phyllis was being fêted. There were meetings with other writers and visits to the theatre. Vera took the appearance of the unworldly Phyllis in hand, turning her from a dowdy woman without make-up into quite a smart figure. Her preoccupation with Phyllis's brilliant career, clothes and social life seems disproportionate and the impression is that Vera was trying in some way to replace Winifred with another Yorkshirewoman who was also a writer. On 6 May, the day Vera collected Phyllis from the station, Winifred wrote from the nursing home,

What a bore it is that they can't yet say when I may leave here. Quite definitely my blood pressure is down and my pulse steadier. But my kidneys are not doing their work and there is a danger if I don't have them put really right now, of getting Bright's Disease or something foul like that. To stop any of these things and make me 100% well . . . means drastic and continual measurements, injections, medicines and diets.

There is no mention of this in Vera's diary, although what Winifred was probably saying, in a reticent Yorkshire way, was that in all probability she did have Bright's Disease (proliferative glomerulonephritis), her kidneys were already badly damaged and that the danger was that treatment would not be able to halt it, the condition being progressive.

Mysteries remain: what did the doctor actually tell Winifred? Did he tell the truth? Did Winifred convey what the doctor told her accurately to Vera? What is obvious, though, is how few questions Vera asked from this point onwards. She had many of the clues required to work out how precarious Winifred's situation might be. She had trained as a nurse and had nursed nephritic soldiers in France. She was a thirty-nine-year-old woman with two children, used to taking questions of health seriously. It looks as if she accepted Winifred's information, or the lack of it, without demanding details. At no point does she seem to have visited the doctor in charge of Winifred's case and asked what was happening. This wilful blindness cannot have been because she did not care; it was because she cared too much and could not bear to hear the truth. This is why, as Winifred lay in the clinic, she failed to record her letter and continued with the arrangements for a party for Phyllis at Glebe Place. Vera Brittain was a woman of courage but probably the one thing in the world she could not face was Winifred's illness. She had seen too many of her contemporaries die. In her early twenties she had lost the two people she had thought would be with her for the rest of her life – her brother and husband-to-be. It had been Winifred who had helped her reshape her life and had always been there afterwards, part-time parent for her children, intellectual companion, confidante, flatmate, friend. The thought that she was failing her now was too much.

She was also in the third year of the work on her book, her first significant bid for attention in the great world. Winifred, being childless, and not ultimately responsible for the household affairs, had been able to leap ahead from the word go, writing her well-thought-of novels, becoming a notable journalist and the youthful director of a national magazine, making friends among the recognized figures of the time. Vera had managed much less and was now facing forty: a grimmer proposition for a woman then than perhaps it is now. She had much less to show for fifteen years of London literary and political life. She was also the supporter of two children, maintained a fairly large house and had responsibility for several servants. Winifred was a major part of her support system – she loved the children, part-owned the house, helped to pay the expenses and engage and deal with the servants. It was she who organized a secretary for Vera and found out why the maid kept crying – she had married secretly and was now pregnant (women's right to work or not, she soon left and was replaced). The thought that Winifred was seriously ill was unendurable, indeed threatening. Small wonder Vera asked so few questions. She could not bear to hear the answers and was no doubt hoping, as we all do on occasions, that if she ignored the situation it might go away.

At first, panic stricken, she threw herself into the relationship with Phyllis Bentley, a kind of surrogate Winifred. There were visits, dressings-up, exchanges of letters and presents, quarrels and reconciliations, all in the manner of teenage girls. Also as with teenage girls, there were jealousies and rivalries. Phyllis had what Vera wanted: success. But Vera had all the other worldly assets: a husband, children, a good life, good looks. Phyllis, literary star and lifelong spinster, seems to have broken down as she told Vera her life at home was very drab and no man had ever made love to her. After one spat between Vera and Phyllis, Winifred, now out of the clinic, remarked with some truth to Vera, 'You've been the most important person in too many people's lives, you little bitch.' Her own position in this affair cannot have been a happy one. She was back at Glebe Place, occupying her own small room, while Phyllis had transferred to George's because he was away. She was on a regular routine of early nights, injections and regular, plain meals, while the much-fêted stranger was being given the best of everything. The door banged continually behind Vera and Phyllis, as the happy pair dressed in their best went out to yet another theatre or party. She must also have been frightened about her health. Yet, of the two, Vera was perhaps the more frightened.

Winifred in fact spent very little of the year at Glebe Place. She went back to Yorkshire in August to rest. She had somehow managed to finish her novel *Mandoa, Mandoa*, in spite of being ill most of the time she was writing it. It is genuinely gay, the only novel she wrote which fully conveys the humour of which she was capable in her journalism. It is a spirited and funny book – perhaps it is true that writers are funnier when, as people, they are saddest. This light-heartedness may have something to do with the fact that the central character is a man; women, in Winifred's books, are not all that happy. They try, life is hard, the outcome often tragic for them. Women, knowing all the problems women face domestically and matrimonially, can easily see the lives of men, or certain kinds of men, as a long series of interesting journeys, meetings and events, all taking place in the big, open, cheerful world outside the home. The central figure of the book, Bill Durrant, is pretty certainly

based on the man Winifred loved, Harry Pearson, who was
indeed always on the move, unsuccessfully, from job to job
and country to country, so it was natural for Winifred to
present the life of her hero like this. This portrait of a kind,
humorous person also explains why Winifred was so fond of
Harry, though he brought her nothing but woe. The book is
satirical – Bill Durrant goes to the invented, uncolonized
African state of Mandoa to build an airport so that his ex-
ploitative boss can bring the country into his orbit and start
up a tourist trap. And although it hinges on what can only
be called culture clashes, including the possibility of slave
raids on Mandoa, it is still true that taking her fiction out of
the known world of the social novel and avoiding the
realities of social, political and sexual realities gave Winifred
the chance to be genuinely funny.

In her own world, the burdens increased. By December
she was caretaking at Glebe Place while Vera lectured in the
North. She stayed on afterwards, since Vera had become
very ill on the tour. When she got back to Yorkshire she
found her father ill and helped at home until he died three
months later. While she was with her mother after her
father's death her aunt became ill and also died.

Both women were now their parents' only surviving
children. Calls on them were many. Winifred was indis-
pensable to Vera, who could not go away without her children unless she left a responsible adult in the house to
supervise everything. At the same time, like Winifred, she
had her parents to consider. As only children, and daughters, both were very vulnerable to family appeals, especially
as neither had the forbidding presence of a husband in the

house to assert his prior claim on them. At about this time Vera began to suffer from bouts of an illness involving sickness, acute pain and fever, which was diagnosed as colo-cystitis. But from the timing of the attacks they appear nervous in origin. A doctor she knew one day gave this as his opinion (the fact that he later killed his wife and was sent to Broadmoor as criminally insane does not completely discredit the diagnosis).

Early in 1933 the still unfinished *Testament of Youth* was bought by Winifred's American publisher Macmillan. In February, after three and a quarter years of work, the book went off to Victor Gollancz, who wrote saying he would be proud to publish it. Vera, although she did not quite know it at the time, was made.

She went to northern France with Winifred, visited the graveyards of the war dead, perhaps feeling the relief of someone who, at last, has paid their tribute in the only way they could; perhaps, also, to see if the ghosts had been finally exorcized. Back in London there were distracted moments of buying clothes and getting photographs taken, in view of possible fame to come. The book was published on 28 August.

The reviews were good, in some cases effusive. The book sold out. The second printing sold out after a fortnight, the third after three weeks. On one day alone in September 5,000 copies were bought. By 1939 sales of the book had reached 120,000 copies. Vera reacted to all this in an unstarry way, managing to get to the TUC Congress at Brighton with George, visiting her parents, taking John off for his first day at school. 'Saw pile of seven or eight copies of *T of Y*,' she records in her diary a fortnight after the publication. 'Sight so unusual for me that I bought a charming hat at Eve Valère's on the strength of it.' Nevertheless, what with attending a huge meeting about the Reichstag trial, going to the PEN Club, broadcasting, arranging for the serialization of the book and generally carrying out a programme which would have killed a horse, she was struck by the familiar gastritis again. She got up and went on. Whether times were good or hard Vera Brittain never showed herself any mercy. During the following year, when by this stage the book had sold 35,000 copies in the USA, she embarked on a lecture tour of the States, giving thirty-four lectures in twenty-five towns across America in the course of three months, a marathon in terms of trains and packing and unpacking. The lecture tour had in fact been offered to both her and Winifred, whose *Mandoa, Mandoa* had also been published in the USA, but it was agreed that because Winifred's health was precarious she would not be able to go, although she could manage to stay behind and take care of matters at Glebe Place. Vera, exhaustedly, enjoyed the tour, which was a proof of fame rather like coast-to-coast chat shows today. Winifred took care of, and sent bulletins about, the children.

It was on this tour, too, that Vera mentions finding her publisher 'attractive'. George Brett ran Macmillan, the firm his father had founded. When he and his wife Isabel paid their annual publisher's visit to London in the summer of 1935 Vera was certainly in love with him. On every level, not just the usual ones, George Brett was irresistible. He was exactly the same age as her, he was rich and powerful, he was the man who had published her book and made her famous in the USA. This was the book where she exorcized the unconsummated love affair with Roland Leighton; George Brett himself had served with the American forces in France in the trenches, and the association between sexual love and death, all centred on those battlefields in France, was still strong.

The short entries in her journal during that summer of 1935, when Vera was forty-one, indicate a love affair. The code of Biblical quotations, always a key to strong emotion, goes on. In June she writes, 'George Brett picked me up after lunch and we talked business, "In my father's house are many mansions."' On a later day in June, after many meetings with George, she quotes St Paul, 'When that which is perfect is come, then that which is in part shall be done away.'

At all events, matters moved quickly that summer. In May Vera was writing her novel *Honourable Estate* at enormous speed. Part of the book concerns the love affair of a young VAD with an American army captain during the First World War. Whether at this stage the book was, so to speak, 'George Brett's book' is debatable. Certainly it seems to have become so afterwards. George Catlin, who had been away studying conditions in Russia under Stalin, came back. His book on politics had been turned down by Cape but almost immediately afterwards, in a Trollopian aside at a party, Ellen Wilkinson, the Labour MP, told Vera that he should 'look out for Sunderland', meaning that there was a chance he might be adopted as Labour candidate for the constituency. Then came the arrival in London of the Bretts and constant meetings between the Bretts and the Catlins, as well as between Vera and George Brett alone. 'At the Savoy I danced with him [George Brett] three times and he had one with practically every other woman guest. Wore my blue and mauve chiffon with the mauve orchids that George [Brett] sent me beforehand,' she reports. And the next day comes the entry, 'When that which is perfect is come . . .' Less than a week later George went to Sunderland for the selection committee and the day after came a telegram saying he had been chosen as prospective candidate for the constituency. Two days later Vera gave a party of 100 guests to celebrate their tenth wedding anniversary and the Bretts, of course, were invited. George Brett contributed a large silver cigarette box engraved in his own handwriting.

It was at some point during this hectic June that Winifred took a room as a study of her own, not far off, in the King's Road. With George Catlin back the house was fuller but it could well be that she thought it was no longer desirable to be at Glebe Place the whole time, and not just because of overcrowding.

At the end of the month she was at the house after supper and, in a conversation which revealed a good deal, finally said to Vera that three years before her doctor had told her that she might have only two years to live. She at last mentioned the time when she had been breaking the ice on the tank for the lambs and heard the phrase from St Paul. Perhaps, with three more months to live, she was trying to warn Vera that she felt less well than she had; perhaps she had had bad news from her doctor; perhaps she wanted to talk about what was happening. We cannot know, there is no record. At any rate, the women do not seem to have talked about this. Vera begged her to write her biography and make its crucial point this experience, 'as I feel it would give courage to many who have lost everything themselves'. It is hard, with hindsight, not to see this response as less than adequate. Winifred may have been asking shyly for help, she may only have been talking about an experience which moved and impressed her. Vera replied by inviting her to write an autobiographical book, when Winifred Holtby was about as likely to write her own life story as a play in Latin verse. But if Vera was deliberately or accidentally missing the point, Winifred was helping her by, deliberately or accidentally, laying a false trail. She had announced several months before that she was planning a trip to West Africa. She was obviously not fit to go, yet everyone had to believe she was, on pain of upsetting her.

If a chance was missed for Vera to talk about Winifred's real feelings about her possible death, Vera made up for it by being remorseless about herself. Perhaps at no point during her life as a consistent autobiographer was she quite so self-critical:

I told her [Winifred] then how I had always felt that she and Gordon (like T. E. Lawrence in a sense) had both hold of a world in which desire and worldly achievement counted for nothing because they had laid hold of the reality beyond life – philosophic truth or whatever one chooses to call it – whereas I am trivial, because I am so much in thrall to my strong earthly desires – for love, for fame, for beauty, for success and also position.

She goes on to say after recording the conversation,

'W[inifred] laid aside desire for love (since Harry had gone), children (since she was told she must never have any), fame (since she thought she would not live to achieve it), How trivial am I, who have all these things, yet never get from them all the happiness I should!' There is self-revelation here but also ambiguity. It is still not clear whether Vera is treating Winifred's renunciations as brave and inevitable, since Winifred was going to die, or whether she is applauding her for being able to make the renunciation when she had to, although it was no longer necessary. It looks on the whole as if Vera discusses Winifred's revelation as an episode from the past, with no bearing on the present. But the grammar makes it unclear. The grammar may reflect her own confusion, even her own desire to conceal her knowledge from herself. Vera was a writer, her greatest success had come through translating her own life into a book, with all the distortion of experience such an exercise is bound to involve. Any writer's life can lead to an unrealistic belief in the power of words. He or she can begin to think that writing is magic; that words, or the lack of them, change reality.

Winifred's Christmas in Yorkshire extended itself. This time her mother was ill. From home she went on to Hornsea, on the Yorkshire coast, to get on with her novel, *South Riding*. She and Vera had a holiday together in Wales and it was not until May that they both returned to London.

Vera had seen the Bretts off at Waterloo on their way to their boat at Southampton. 'Determined to seem gay, and did,' she declares, but George Brett simply told her he was tired and would never return to Britain for a month again. He would either come for a longer, or a shorter, time. Then he shook hands with her and gave her a long look, the meaning of which she could not interpret. That evening she records, 'Slowly to bed, wondering if it was the end or not.'

She cannot have felt particularly cheerful when, a month later, she, the governess and a family friend set off for Normandy, taking John and Shirley on their first trip abroad. Her husband was due later, Winifred later still. Three days after their arrival they were having lunch at the hotel when John, always Winifred's greatest fan, spotted her coming through the lounge to meet them. Vera knew immediately that something was wrong. Those who had lived through the First World War had learned to dread telegrams, always the first news that someone had been killed. Winifred, to spare Vera the sight of a telegram, had taken the journey from England to break some bad news in person – Vera's father had disappeared early in the morning the day before and had still not been found. The immediate suspicion was that he, who suffered from depression and often talked of suicide, had killed himself. Vera and Winifred, who was in a state of collapse after the journey, set off straight away, arriving in London at midnight. Two days later Thomas Brittain's body was found in the Thames at Twickenham. Winifred went to Yorkshire but George was there to identify the body and be present at the inquest and the funeral. Vera feared the publicity which would result if the papers linked her father with his famous daughter – suicide was considered a family disgrace in those days – but George spoke to some of the newspapers and there was almost no mention of the matter. Meanwhile the children were still in Normandy and the day after the funeral George became seriously ill with glandular poisoning. Vera must have panicked. She had said goodbye to her lover, her father had just drowned himself, now it looked as if her husband might die. She had sustained the loss of the male figures in her life twenty years before and would not be able to bear it again.

So, although according to Vera's later autobiography, *Testament of Experience*, Winifred was still in France with the children, in fact she came down from Yorkshire and Vera, in what can only be described as a perfunctory way, allowed her to go over to France and stay with the children while she nursed her husband back to health. Off went the ill but conscientious friend, coming back at the end of August looking fit and well. And a week later was 'very ill and tired'. Meanwhile Vera did what energetic and self-demanding people do during and after exhausting crises: she went into overdrive, piling one small task on another – visiting an aunt who had had an operation in Chichester, going to a publisher's party, interviewing a new agent. Winifred became more ill and was transferred to a nursing home. Vera still could not see Winifred's doctor. It was George who did so and heard that five years before, progress of renal sclerosis, a hardening of the tissues of the kidneys, had advanced so far that they were only performing about a quarter of their normal function. Having been told then that she might have only two years to live, she had defied the calculations and the doctor still held out some hope that she could defeat the inevitable. George and Vera cancelled their projected holiday in Monte Carlo (it is fortunate

Winifred collapsed when she did, rather than later, when she would undoubtedly have been in charge of the children). Instead they went down to Brighton, in order to be within call, while carrying on pretending to Winifred that her condition was not so serious that they dared not go away. Poor Vera, who had waited for Roland in a Brighton hotel twenty years before, was again in Brighton, waiting. The call came. They returned.

Among the many people present in the sitting-room of Winifred's clinic were Clare Leighton, the redoubtable Lady Rhondda, who behaved impeccably, Alice Holtby, of course, and Vera, naturally. The last three constitute the trio of women most important in Winifred's life. Vera, her friend, Alice Holtby, her mother, and Lady Rhondda, her employer. Later Vera was to accuse Lady Rhondda of overworking and exploiting Winifred; Alice Holtby thought the same of Vera. All three women seem to have thought the same about each other and to a certain extent they were all probably guilty – Vera admitted as much. These days we would probably be quicker to blame the victim, Winifred, for allowing them all to make too many claims on her; we might argue that her need to be needed tempted the others to exploit her. This may be partially true, but we have to remember that however un-Christian people at that time might have thought themselves, they were not nearly so un-Christian as we are. Much of the old ethic of self-sacrifice and lack of self-interest as the highest good still remained. The concept of personal fulfilment as a virtue did not exist. Winifred, who considered herself always lucky and privileged, felt that she really owed service to those less fortunate than herself, that it was her duty to help where she could. Years later even Amy Burnett, the housekeeper at Glebe Place (and a living-in housekeeper does not always see her employers at their best) recalled Winifred as 'an angel'. Neither Alice Holtby, nor Vera Brittain, nor Lady Rhondda were 'angels'. According to their natures, they asked; according to hers, Winifred gave, and she never seems to have grudged the giving.

Grotesque scenes appear to have taken place in the sitting-room at the clinic as mother and best friend battled over the sick woman, violating each other's sense of what was right and proper. Mrs Holtby was already planning the funeral and opening Winifred's will. Vera contacted the press to say that Winifred was ill, in order to publicize her as a writer and, presumably, not as Alderwoman Holtby's daughter. 'No more,' pleaded Mrs Holtby. There was even competition between them over who should see Winifred first after she died (Vera won, by a ruse). It was probably the end of a long battle for who should possess the most of Winifred. The conversations extended even to the funeral arrangements, before Winifred was dead.

At least Winifred did not know about the battles between these two very distressed women. And Vera redressed the balance in her own favour at the last moment. She made it possible for Winifred to die happy. A few days previously Vera had sent a telegram to Harry Pearson saying that Winifred wanted to see him. He came and sat up with her for several nights, giving her great comfort. Then Winifred, who must by then have been under heavy sedation, began to say how much she wanted to marry him. 'I decided,' says Vera, 'that the one thing she still wanted to make her life complete she must have, and that Harry must be persuaded to play his part before it was too late.'

With her usual admirable promptitude she cornered George and asked him if he would tell Harry to ask Winifred to marry him. That evening George and Harry had dinner together. George asked Harry; he agreed. In fact he told George he had always thought he and Winifred would marry in the end. It was the contrast between Winifred's good career and his disastrous one, and, it seems, the fact that he had never been passionately attracted to her as a woman, which had always held him back.

Winifred's time was running out, so next day Vera sent a message to Harry to come quickly. She conspired with Lady Rhondda to keep Alice Holtby out of the way while Harry paid his visit to Winifred. Vera discreetly disappeared into a café while George kept watch at the clinic to make sure nothing went wrong. Finally Harry appeared and went into the clinic, George then slipped across the road and joined Vera in the café. When Lady Rhondda brought Alice Holtby across to the same café for tea and conversation, George and Vera went unseen down to the basement. Then Alice Holtby went back to hear her daughter say how happy she was that she and Harry were engaged. Vera never heard Winifred's account from her own lips, though she dearly wanted to. The doctor found Winifred so elated that he ordered a very heavy dose of morphine for her and she went into a coma from which she never recovered. Vera, called in by prior arrangement with the night sister, was with her in the early morning, holding her hand, as she died without recovering consciousness.

The next day George left Vera in the care of the novelist Storm Jameson and went down to Brighton to speak at the Labour Party Conference. He was a prospective candidate now and there was no doubt, as they said, that Winifred would have wanted him to go. But it is perhaps a sign of how semi-detached the marriage had become that at this moment he did not stay with Vera, or that she did not go with him.

FOUR

The Second World War

It was to be over a year before Vera began *Testament of Friendship,* her tribute to Winifred Holtby, and three years before she finished it. In November she went up to Sunderland to support her husband in his election campaign. Defeat followed. 'Our third major catastrophe this year,' she wrote to a friend. By the end of 1935, though, the election defeat forgotten, she was saying with her usual clear-headedness and all the weariness of a woman in her forties who has gone through too many crises in too short a space of time, 'Winifred in dying took with her that second life that she initiated for me after the War; can I make a third? Can I, once more, begin again? Are children and books enough incentive for living?'

It was in this year that she saw through to publication the manuscript Winifred had completed, but obviously had not prepared for the press. *South Riding* is Winifred's best-known book. It is strongly in the tradition of the provincial social novel. This time she does not deal with rural Yorkshire, but with the Yorkshire of town and country. Linking the events of the whole tale are the dealings of the South

Riding County Council. South Riding is, of course, an imaginary area. At the time Yorkshire was divided into three administrative areas, or 'ridings' (from the old word 'thirdings'), East, West and North. *South Riding* is set around the town of Kingsport, where the poor live in caravans, the bourgeoisie in solid brick houses and the landed gentry in manors in the surrounding countryside. The whole society is there: squire, aldermen, grocers, publicans, farmers, the honest and the dishonest, the conservative and the progressive, the old, the young and the middle-aged. The two main characters are the local landowner, Robert Carne – handsome, profoundly conservative and married to a mad wife with whom he will never again be able to live – and Sarah Burton – young, radical, a schoolmistress at a girls' school. The other two dominant characters are girls: the lonely Midge Carne, Robert Carne's daughter, and clever Lydia Holly, who is destined to leave school, her promise unfulfilled, because she is the oldest girl in a big, poor family and her mother, worn out by bearing and rearing too many children, is going to die. The love affair which develops between Robert Carne and Sarah Burton fails a little to convince, Carne being too much the damaged but devastatingly attractive figure beloved of romantic novelists to fit well in a social novel crowded with sharply individual, everyday characters. It is, in fact, the sense of life and action which holds the book together. Winifred Holtby's women, in her novels, are always left sad. Sarah Burton, like Mary Robson in *Anderby Wold* and Joanna Burton in *The Land of Green Ginger*, ends with only stoical courage, determination and hope to carry her on. It is sad that this is Winifred Holtby's last book; impossible to imagine what she might have done if, as she matured, an artistic selfishness had taken over and she had kept more time for herself, and had been able to count on a future.

In the following year Vera completed her own book, *Honourable Estate*, begun when matters seemed so much more hopeful. She was now an established writer in her forties, with her children growing up healthy and happy, and, as a result of her earnings and money left to her by her father, the owner of a country cottage and a large house in Cheyne Walk, Chelsea overlooking the river. As the 1930s went on she ought to have started a new and happy life. Yet Winifred's death must have shorn off part of herself, and the prospect of war made contentment harder and harder to achieve.

In the spring of 1936 Vera and George visited Germany, as Hitler, already Führer, won the election by 99 per cent of the votes. They seem merely to have gone to witness the facts, under no illusions about the motives and intentions of the régime. During this trip Vera was at her best, observing with political sense and with a sharp Buxtonite eye for the betraying detail. After going to hear Hitler speak she says,

[His voice] begins by being so clear, sonorous, and impressive, though it begins to crack and shrill when he gets emotional. At the same time he clenches his fist and beats his breast like a penitent in an agony of religious fervour. Did not strike me as a wily diplomatist but a religious maniac.

In one of the only two cafés in Frankfurt where Jews were

.d she noted 'a collective sense of humiliation among patrons'. She felt 'as if I were among a gathering of .rondins under the terror – or prisoners of war – or exiles in a foreign country'. She notes the wife of the British Vice-consul in Frankfurt as saying Hitler had become more gentle-manly in his behaviour over the past few years. On one occasion she holds a German map up to the light and spots that the café with the pasted-over name has a Jewish owner, on another she checks the place on a building where a commemorative plaque to a distinguished Jew has been taken off and tidily replastered. 'The régime is nothing if not thorough,' she remarks.

In retrospect none of this is very remarkable, but it has to be recalled that although many British people knew of, and deplored, what was happening in Germany, many, often the wealthy and influential, were more tolerant. Anti-Semitism, an age-old European vice, did not stop at the Channel – Jews were still discriminated against in Britain. It was quite possible to see Hitler's acts as comprehensible if a little too drastic, but Vera has no hesitation about condemning what was going on.

Faced with the prospect of a second war with Germany, what were the pacifists – Quakers, other Christians and the vast army of witnesses to the carnage of the First World War – to do? The League of Nations on which they had pinned their hopes had not brought the countries of Europe together. Some pacifists lost faith. Another generation, which had not experienced, first hand, the bitterness of the war, had grown up. But there was still enough active anti-war feeling in the country for the Peace Pledge Union, founded in 1934 by a Church of England clergyman, Canon Dick Sheppard, to have attracted about 100,000 supporters by 1936, each of whom had signed the Peace Pledge: 'I remember war and never again will I support or sanction another and I will do all in my power to persuade others to do the same.' By 1937 130,000 people had signed the Pledge and had it not been for the unexpected death in that year of the charismatic and endearing Canon Dick Sheppard, the movement might have been even more influential as the Second World War approached.

The Peace Pledge Union was not a political movement. It was more concerned with bearing personal witness, rather like the Greenham Common Women, than with pushing for political change, but obviously if the majority of people supported it the country could not go to war. Vera became a sponsor. In a way, she had no choice. It is no surprise that later her daughter remembers her mother, in her sixties, being carried away by policemen on a CND demonstration. Those who had seen the landscape of northern France saw in miniature some of the worst scenes we vaguely imagine about the fringes of a nuclear war: a landscape flattened and reduced to stumps of trees and piles of bricks, the wounded lying for days without help, the dead unrecovered and unburied, the survivors facing a world of the dead and mutilated. Small wonder Vera decided to add her support to the large numbers joining Dick Sheppard then, and CND later. But the Peace Pledge Union said implicitly that man's efforts towards peace would fail without God. Vera's later pacifist writings are certainly Christian in tone. In *Humiliation with Honour*, published in 1942, she likens the desire for war to a drop of poison left in the blood by Lucifer. Her prose is often emotionally religious, almost religiose. There is no explanation of how this woman, whose adherence to the Church of England, that least religious of faiths, appears previously to have been fairly nominal, whose earlier writings show little evidence of faith and whose portrait of the clergy high and low in *Honourable Estate* is not flattering, can have become quite such a Christian. Nevertheless, she had never quite abandoned faith. Like many she had turned to God in moments of high emotion, such as those caused by love and death. Perhaps she was calling on that deeply romantic, sentimental and unintellectual layer beneath the repressed and agnostic surface of the British, or perhaps just English, character, which tends to surface when all is lost, ships are sinking and the battle nearly lost. Then the beauty of biblical prose and the stirring words and tunes of *Hymns Ancient and Modern* come to mind. Strike leaders and football teams are serenaded by hymn tunes. It may have been the British God, always there when you need him (unlike the British policeman), whom Vera saw as the only answer, now, to war.

Nevertheless, if the Peace Pledge Union had at least the respectability of being headed by a clergyman of the Established Church, having to join openly was a sacrifice for Vera. She was not a committed rebel whose satisfaction came from always being in opposition. Her conscience guided her towards positions which challenged the establishment, the old order, but she had a strong desire for public recognition and approval. Membership of the Peace Pledge Union was not going to bring her closer to acceptance by the official establishment or even by very many of the official counter-establishment. As she says twenty years later in *Testament of Experience*, 'For three years now I had enjoyed outstanding success in different parts of the world ... Everything in me recoiled from the prospect of exchanging this welcome stimulus for public disapproval.' Her position was to be somewhat salvaged later, as it turned out, but she could not have known that at the time.

It was as she completed *Honourable Estate* that George Brett arrived for his annual visit. Her diary entries for that time read comparatively flatly. Perhaps the relationship was not progressing, although having come round to collect one chapter – in which the American Captain makes love to the British VAD – they spent the whole afternoon discussing the dialogue. (Since this chapter occurs half-way through the book, which Vera was on the verge of finishing, her motives in offering him just this portion must have been mixed.) This time, true to his words as he left the previous year, he did only spend a short time in Britain: a fortnight. As he was leaving, Vera writes, quoting *Story of an African Farm*, the book which had haunted her since she was first given it by Roland Leighton, '"Sometimes such a sudden gladness seizes me when I remember that somewhere you are living and working."'

But *Honourable Estate* was not just the product, so to speak, of a love affair. In my opinion it is the only novel of Vera Brittain's which has stood the test of time, although it is now out of print. It is also the longest. It is divided into three parts, the first being the life of Janet Rutherston, unhappily married to a clergyman and mother of one son,

Denis. The second part concerns the Alleyndene family, who have a daughter, Ruth. The third part brings both children, Denis Rutherston and Ruth Alleyndene, together and eventually they marry.

Janet Rutherston is the sad portrait of a woman with aspirations to social and political action, crushed by marriage to a weak and conservative husband, a clergyman older than herself, who does not understand what she wants and exerts his authority to make her conform. It is a picture, too, of a desperately unhappy marriage. The child, Denis, is brought up in the misery of domestic conflict, watching his mother being slowly crushed.

In the parish of Witnall the Alleyndenes, the most important local family, force Thomas Rutherston out of the parish. The Alleyndenes are a rich, proud, philistine family, who must have been based on Vera's idea of her own. Old Enoch Alleyndene, a violent and intransigent man, pushes his wife out of the carriage during a row. His kindly son has an arrangement with the local tobacconist's wife, which his wife pretends not to know about. In her pew she reflects as she hears the vicar read, 'We brought nothing into this world and it is certain we can carry nothing out,' that 'The Alleyndenes didn't really believe in that democratic exhortation. They came into the world inheriting lands and dividends and they went out leaving their descendants to fight their way through a barbed-wire entanglement of entails and trusts.' The daughter of the family, Ruth, goes to Oxford, but on the day she is told she has been given a first-class degree the news comes that her brother has been killed at Gallipoli. She goes to France to nurse as a VAD and is found by Eugene Meury, son of American newspaper owners, who was a soldier at Gallipoli with her brother. He brings her a letter in which her brother tells Ruth that in order to survive the horrors of the war he and his school friend, who was expelled from school for homosexuality, have become lovers. Faced with a possible court martial, they may decide to make sure they are killed. Ruth is shocked by this but accepts it. She and Eugene Meury fall in love. Forgetting the rules by which she was brought up, she becomes his lover. He is later killed in battle.

Denis Rutherston and Ruth Alleyndene meet in Russia, where he is on a committee investigating the famine which followed the Revolution, she is nursing during the typhoid epidemic. They fall in love and marry, and because Ruth wants more than the life of a wife and mother of the times, and Denis, having witnessed his parents' unhappy marriage, would never make his wife miserable by restricting her, they achieve a union where both are happy. Ruth is finally elected to Parliament for the Labour Party in the constituency where her family once held sway, and where Denis's father was thrown out of his parish.

The book has more solidity and drive, a better construction and more genuine feeling than any novel Vera Brittain wrote before or was to write later. The solidly biographical nature of much of the material must have buoyed up a writer more interested in biography and autobiography than fiction. Vera's introduction denies that there is any biographical or autobiographical content, but George Catlin's father was, like Denis Rutherston's, a clergyman, and the Alleyndenes appear to be a semi-portrait of the tains. Other autobiographical connections, like Ruth Aleyndene's nursing in France, hardly need to be stressed. Vera's claim in the Introduction (and in the subtitle of the book: 'A Novel of Transition') that she is partly recording the changes in women's lives during the period 1894–1930 is true and she manages to demonstrate, in fiction, the actuality of those changes. In *Honourable Estate* she manages to close the gap between autobiography, social comment and imagination, which so often she was unable to do.

By now a declared pacifist, both she and George Catlin had criticized Hitler. If Britain were faced with invasion, their position might become very dangerous. She and George had to conclude that she could not leave the children in England to share their possible fate if either or both of them intended to stay. They could easily have gone to America, where they had friends and connections. But somehow the idea of Vera Brittain leaving the country in time of war was ludicrous. In the event, both George and Vera stayed. John and Shirley, aged twelve and nine, left to stay with friends in Minnesota, though, like so many parents of evacuated children, George and Vera did not stick to their decision to the very end. In 1943, as soon as an Allied victory seemed certain, the children came home again.

The decision to send the children out of the country and remain herself was a difficult one for Vera, but other decisions were easier. With her usual speed in combining thought with action she decided in 1939 that the only possibility for a pacifist in time of war was to fight, intellectually, for her ideas. She decided to produce a pacifist newsletter, supported by subscribers. She did so on a weekly basis at first and then, as the paper shortage became a problem, fortnightly, not only until the end of the war, but for two years after it. It says a great deal for her persistence, the liberality of a government at war and probably the strength of her own reputation that she was not only permitted to do this, but also to publish what could have been regarded as pacifist propaganda – *Humiliation with Honour* – in the middle of the conflict.

Although the book was not censored, it was rumoured that there was a Home Office dossier on her, meaning that she was possibly considered unreliable. She was triumphantly vindicated, however, when it was proved that all along she had been on Hitler's black list of people to be arrested, and probably eliminated, in the event of a German occupation of Britain. Even better for her reputation at the time must have been the fact that her name appeared on the same page as that of Winston Churchill – the list was alphabetical – and so was frequently published. There could have been no better publicity for a possible dangerous subversive, though a cynic might wonder if it is not the normal fate of a pacifist to be mistrusted by both sides.

Meanwhile, the blitz started. Vera was alone in London, her children gone and George lecturing in the USA. He left boldly in July 1941 but it was possible he might not be able to return, or, if he tried, he might be on a ship attacked by submarines. At a certain point he cabled to Vera, 'Go immediately to Lakes', meaning that she should take shelter with relatives in Westmorland. Vera, in Portland Place, right in the middle of the London bombing, says in *Testament of Experience* that she thought,

Safe areas were no part of my scheme for living; normal life, comfortable and unthreatened, now seemed as abnormal as bombs had once appeared and contributed nothing to a book about the war. Nor, from the security of a relative's home, amid lakes and mountains, could I write fortnightly letters for readers under bombardment.

In the event she not only stayed, but was tireless. There was the newsletter. She sat on a tribunal screening conscientious objectors. She worked for the Children's Overseas Reception Board, which was arranging for children to be sent out of danger to Commonwealth countries. For her documentary book, *England's Hour*, she went out on duty at night with the ARP (air-raid precautions), she visited reception centres for bombed-out families, she toured the shattered East End and the City of London. Her sharp and specific eye even recorded her own house, hastily evacuated until a nearby delayed-action bomb had exploded:

The clocks have all stopped ticking ... a profound silence greets me from the empty rooms ... all over the stairs the bomb has shaken down dust and plaster ... On the floor of my study at the top of the empty house lie piles of books which Robert was about to clean with the vacuum cleaner when the time-bomb fell; amongst them the vacuum cleaner had fallen drunkenly ...

Then George returned, but only after the ship he was on had been torpedoed. He spent eight hours in a lifeboat in the middle of the Atlantic in December. 'Slight mishap shipwreck open boat eight hours entirely safe but in pyjamas,' he cabled in true British fashion. And so the Brittain–Catlins stayed on in Britain, mostly in London, for the rest of the war, enduring much of the bombing. George

Catlin lectured to the forces, Vera to civilians all over the country, including some of the worst-hit cities – Coventry, Birmingham, Plymouth.

Vera was to live until 1970, write further books and become involved in the third movement in her lifetime which represented aspirations towards peace: the Campaign for Nuclear Disarmament. But perhaps it is fitting that our final picture is of Vera Brittain in 1942, at the age of forty-eight, on what she called evening shelter work, this time going through the streets with a Quaker team, serving soup to a thousand people in improvised shelters under the railway arches of East London. 'My passion for experience, perpetually at odds with my natural cowardice, had again come out on top,' she writes drily about her experiences during the blitz. She does not mention her other natural passions, like the passion for doing something constructive to counter destruction or for going quickly where her active conscience led. The vision of this small, middle-aged woman standing, for a second time, in the ruins created by war, doing something practical, readying herself to write about it so that other people could know what it was like, is not just impressive, but very touching. Her determination, resolution, sheer physical courage and her insistence on bearing witness to what happened – those are the qualities she perhaps never valued sufficiently in herself, but they are the qualities for which we most remember her.

FIVE

Postscript

Vera Brittain went on to write many other books, among them two further novels and *Testament of Experience*, the continuation of her autobiography. She died in 1970 at the age of 76. Her husband, Sir George Catlin, was knighted in 1970, remarried in 1971 and died in 1979. Their son John Catlin is a marketing consultant and painter. Their daughter, Shirley Williams, was first elected to Parliament in 1964, was a member of the Labour Cabinet from 1974 to 1979 and is co-founder of the SDP and its first elected MP.

SELECT BIBLIOGRAPHY

Books by Vera Brittain

Verses of a VAD, Erskine Macdonald (1918)
The Dark Tide (novel), Grant Richards (1923)
Not Without Honour (novel), Grant Richards (1924)
Woman's Work in Modern Britain, Noel Douglas (1928)
Halcyon, or The Future of Monogamy, Kegan Paul & Co. (1929)
Testament of Youth, Victor Gollancz (1933), Fontana Paperbacks in
    association with Virago (1979), Seaview Books (1980), Wide-
    view Books (1981)
Poems of the War and After, Victor Gollancz (1934)
Honourable Estate (novel), Victor Gollancz (1936)
Thrice a Stranger, Victor Gollancz (1938)
Testament of Friendship, Macmillan & Co. (1940), Virago (1980),
    Virago and Fontana (1981)
War-time Letters to Peace Lovers, Peace Book Co. (1940)
England's Hour, Macmillan & Co. (1941), Futura (1980)
Humiliation with Honour, Andrew Dakers (1942)
Account Rendered (novel), Macmillan & Co. (1945), Virago (1982)
On Becoming a Writer, Hutchinson (1947)
Born 1925 (novel), Macdonald & Co. (1948), Virago (1982)
Search after Sunrise, Macmillan & Co. (1951)
Lady into Woman, Andrew Dakers (1953)
Testament of Experience, Victor Gollancz (1957), Virago (1979)

VERA BRITTAIN

Envoy Extraordinary: A Study of Vijaya Lakshmi Pandit, George Allen
   & Unwin (1965)
Radclyffe Hall: A Case of Obscenity?, Femina Books (1968)
Chronicle of Youth (journal), Victor Gollancz (1981)
Chronicle of Friendship (journal), Victor Gollancz (1986)

FOR THE BEST IN PAPERBACKS, LOOK FOR THE

In every corner of the world, on every subject under the sun, Penguins represent quality and variety – the very best in publishing today.

For complete information about books available from Penguin and how to order them, write to us at the appropriate address below. Please note that for copyright reasons the selection of books varies from country to country.

In the United Kingdom: For a complete list of books available from Penguin in the U.K., please write to *Dept EP, Penguin Books Ltd, Harmondsworth, Middlesex, UB7 0DA*

In the United States: For a complete list of books available from Penguin in the U.S., please write to *Dept BA, Viking Penguin, 299 Murray Hill Parkway, East Rutherford, New Jersey 07073*

In Canada: For a complete list of books available from Penguin in Canada, please write to *Penguin Books Canada Limited, 2801 John Street, Markham, Ontario L3R 1B4*

In Australia: For a complete list of books available from Penguin in Australia, please write to the *Marketing Department, Penguin Books Australia Ltd, P.O. Box 257, Ringwood, Victoria 3134*

In New Zealand: For a complete list of books available from Penguin in New Zealand, please write to the *Marketing Department, Penguin Books (N.Z.) Ltd, Private Bag, Takapuna, Auckland 9*

In India: For a complete list of books available from Penguin in India, please write to *Penguin Overseas Ltd, 706 Eros Apartments, 56 Nehru Place, New Delhi 110019*

PENGUIN MODERN CLASSICS

Death of a Salesman Arthur Miller

One of the great American plays of the century, this classic study of failure brings to life an unforgettable character: Willy Loman, the shifting and inarticulate hero who is nonetheless a unique individual.

The Echoing Grove Rosamund Lehmann

'No English writer has told of the pains of women in love more truly or more movingly than Rosamund Lehmann' – Marghenita Laski. 'This novel is one of the most absorbing I have read for years' – Simon Raven, *Listener*

Pale Fire Vladimir Nabokov

This book contains the last poem by John Slade, together with a Preface, notes and Index by his posthumous editor. But is the eccentric editor more than just haughty and intolerant – mad, bad, perhaps even dangerous . . .?

The Man Who Was Thursday G. K. Chesterton

This hilarious extravaganza concerns a secret society of revolutionaries sworn to destroy the world. But when Thursday turns out to be not a poet but a Scotland Yard detective, one starts to wonder about the identity of the others . . .

The Rebel Albert Camus

Camus's 'attempt to understand the time I live in' tries to justify innocence in an age of atrocity. 'One of the vital works of our time, compassionate and disillusioned, intelligent but instructed by deeply felt experience' – *Observer*

Letters to Milena Franz Kafka

Perhaps the greatest collection of love letters written in the twentieth century, they are an orgy of bliss and despair, of ecstasy and desperation poured out by Kafka in his brief two-year relationship with Milena Jesenska.

The Age of Reason   Jean-Paul Sartre

The first part of Sartre's classic trilogy, set in the volatile Paris summer of 1938, is itself 'a dynamic, deeply disturbing novel' (Elizabeth Bowen) which tackles some of the major issues of our time.

Three Lives   Gertrude Stein

A turning point in American literature, these portraits of three women – thin, worn Anna, patient, gentle Lena and the complicated, intelligent Melanctha – represented in 1909 one of the pioneering examples of modernist writing.

Doctor Faustus   Thomas Mann

Perhaps the most convincing description of an artistic genius ever written, this portrait of the composer Leverkuhn is a classic statement of one of Mann's obsessive themes: the discord between genius and sanity.

The New Machiavelli   H. G. Wells

This autobiography of a man who has thrown up a glittering political career and marriage to go into exile with the woman he loves also contains an illuminating Introduction by Melvyn Bragg.

The Collected Poems of Stevie Smith

Amused, amusing and deliciously barbed, this volume includes many poems which dwell on death; as a whole, though, as this first complete edition in paperback makes clear, Smith's poetry affirms an irrepressible love of life.

Rhinoceros / The Chairs / The Lesson   Eugène Ionesco

Three great plays by the man who was one of the founders of what has come to be known as the Theatre of the Absurd.

The Second Sex   Simone de Beauvoir

This great study of Woman is a landmark in feminist history, drawing together insights from biology, history and sociology as well as literature, psychoanalysis and mythology to produce one of the supreme classics of the twentieth century.

The Bridge of San Luis Rey   Thornton Wilder

On 20 July 1714 the finest bridge in all Peru collapsed, killing 5 people. Why? Did it reveal a latent pattern in human life? In this beautiful, vivid and compassionate investigation, Wilder asks some searching questions in telling the story of the survivors.

Parents and Children   Ivy Compton-Burnett

This richly entertaining introduction to the world of a unique novelist brings to light the deadly claustrophobia within a late-Victorian upper-middle-class family . . .

Vienna 1900   Arthur Schnitzler

These deceptively languid sketches, four 'games with love and death', lay bare an astonishing and disturbing world of sexual turmoil (which anticipates Freud's discoveries) beneath the smooth surface of manners and convention.

Confessions of Zeno   Italo Svevo

Zeno, an innocent in a corrupt world, triumphs in the end through his stoic acceptance of his own failings in this extraordinary, experimental novel which fuses memory, obsession and desire.

The House of Mirth   Edith Wharton

Lily Bart – beautiful, intelligent and charming – is trapped like a butterfly in the inverted jam jar of wealthy New York society . . . This tragic comedy of manners was one of Wharton's most shocking and innovative books

FOR THE BEST IN PAPERBACKS, LOOK FOR THE 🐧

PENGUIN LITERARY BIOGRAPHIES

Sylvia Beach and the Lost Generation   Noel Riley Fitch
Arnold Bennett   Margaret Drabble
Elizabeth Bowen   Victoria Glendinning
Joseph Conrad   Jocelyn Baines
Scott Fitzgerald   André Le Vot
The Young Thomas Hardy   Robert Gittings
Ibsen   Michael Meyer
John Keats   Robert Gittings
Jack Kerouac: Memory Babe – A Critical Biography   Gerald Nicosia
Ezra Pound   Noel Stock
Dylan Thomas   Paul Ferris
Tolstoy   Henri Troyat
Evelyn Waugh   Christopher Sykes
Walt Whitman   Paul Zweig
Oscar Wilde   Hesketh Pearson

FOR THE BEST IN PAPERBACKS, LOOK FOR THE 🐧

THE PENGUIN LIVES AND LETTERS SERIES

A series of diaries and letters, journals and memoirs

William Allingham: A Diary, 1824–1889   Introduced by John Julius Norwich

Arnold Bennett: The Journals   Edited by Frank Swinnerton

Lord Byron: Selected Letters and Journals   Edited by Peter Gunn

The Daughters of Karl Marx: Family Correspondence 1866–98   With a Commentary and Notes by Olga Meier

Earthly Paradise   Colette

The Letters of Rachel Henning   Edited by David Adams with a Foreword and Drawings by Norman Lindsay

Lord Hervey's Memoirs   Edited by Romney Sedgwick

Julia: A Portrait of Julia Strachey   By Herself and Frances Partridge

Memoirs of the Forties   By Julian Maclaren-Ross, with a new Introduction by Alan Ross

Harold Nicolson: Diaries and Letters: 1930–64   Edited and Condensed by Stanley Olson

The Pastons: The Letter of a Family in the Wars of the Roses   Edited by Richard Barber

Queen Victoria in her Letters and Journals   A Selection by Christopher Hibbert

The Quest for Corvo: An Experiment in Biography   By A. J. A. Symons

Saint-Simon at Versailles   Selected and Translated from the Memoirs of M. le Duc de Saint-Simon by Lucy Norton

Osbert Sitwell: Left Hand, Right Hand!   Abridged and Introduced by Patrick Taylor-Martin

Evelyn Waugh: Diaries   Edited by Michael Davie

LIVES OF MODERN WOMEN

Titles already published, or in preparation

Hannah Arendt Derwent May

Simone de Beauvoir Lisa Appignanesi

Annie Besant Rosemary Dinnage

Elizabeth Bowen Patricia Craig

Vera Brittain Hilary Bailey

Coco Chanel Diane Johnson

Colette Allan Massie

Margaret Mead Phyllis Grosskurth

Christabel and Sylvia Pankhurst Barbara Castle

Sylvia Plath Anne Stevenson

Jean Rhys Carole Angier

Bessie Smith Elaine Feinstein

Freya Stark Caroline Moorehead

Mme Sun Yat Sen Jung Chang

Marina Tsetsayeva Elaine Feinstein

Rebecca West Fay Weldon